EARRINGS

Rizzoli NEW YORK

over 600 examples
108 in colour

DANIELA MASCETTI
AMANDA TRIOSSI

RINGS

from antiquity to the present

First published in the United States of America in 1990 by
Rizzoli International Publications, Inc.
300 Park Avenue South, New York, NY 10010

Library of Congress Cataloging-in-Publication Data

Mascetti, Daniela.
    Earrings : from antiquity to the present / Daniela Mascetti,
Amanda Triossi.
        p.   cm.
    ISBN 0-8478-1230-8
    1. Earrings—History. I. Triossi, Amanda. II. Title.
GT2263.M36 1990
391'.7—dc20   90-52600
                                                        CIP

Printed and bound in Singapore by CS Graphics

CONTENTS

TO
ADALISA
ANTHEA
GIUSEPPE
LUIGI

Preface

Earlobes, necks, wrists and fingers are among the chief parts of the human anatomy which lend themselves to applied decoration. As with so many innovations in the field of jewellery, the practice of piercing the fleshy protuberances of the ears for the attachment of ornaments symbolic of race, tribe and status seems to have originated in Western Asia. A sculptured slab from the palace of Ashurnasirpal II (883–859 BC) in the British Museum depicts the king in profile wearing a long earring with an acorn-shaped terminal. At various stages of history men, women and children have been subjected to the ordeal of ear-piercing, though the male fashion for earrings has been mysteriously intermittent and sometimes a national rather than a cultural phenomenon.

English courtiers adorned themselves with single pearl drop earrings in the late 16th and early 17th centuries but some hundred and fifty years later, when similar ornaments were worn by French officers, the vogue aroused astonishment and hilarity in England. Thomas Rowlandson capitalized on the reaction in 1786 with a cartoon showing French officers in various stages of donning their uniforms; they all sport earrings. Eleven years later the diarist Mrs Lybbe-Powys was struck by the sight of a French *emigré* officer in Bath 'with large gold earrings'. But for all the British distaste, the custom had become general in France and Italy, from the highest to the lowest. Napoleon himself did not wear them, but his brother-in-law Joachim Murat, whom he made King of Naples in 1808, undoubtedly did. In the mid-1970s, when the fashion recurred, young Englishmen were among the most enthusiastic proponents of the emblematic use of a single earring.

There is no evidence of the methods employed to pierce ears in prehistoric times but references in more recent centuries establish that the well-to-do employed the services of professional jewellers when the girls in the family were considered old enough to wear earrings. The experience for the victims was usually made palatable by the prospect of possessing a pair of ornaments of their very own. But even that prize was sometimes insufficient. The august presence of a royal jeweller, Dutens, summoned by Mrs Delany to attend her niece Mary Dewes in 1756, failed to persuade the young girl to submit to the operation. She held out for two months before succumbing. Girls of less affluent families were subjected to amateur attention with the aid of a needle, which pierced the ear while the lobe was supported by a piece of wood or other solid material. A cork was popular in the 19th century and later.

Children were dressed as miniature adults until the late 19th century and the ornaments worn by girls reflected contemporary fashions. There are comparatively few breaks in the history of female earrings charted by the authors, the longest being the Middle Ages, when the fashion for swathed heads concealed not only the hair but the ears as well. In the late 16th century women showed a renewed interest in ear ornaments, especially in the pearl drops which predominated for the next century and a half and survived thereafter. They were far more comfortable to wear than the girandole earrings which rivalled the drop type from the late 17th century. Usually comprising a top, an intermediate device such as a bow and three (or more) drops, these articles were so heavy that a secondary loop was often attached to the hook which passed through the ear and a ribbon threaded to the hook to be secured to the hair, taking some of the weight off the ears. This device helped, but many women reduced the period of discomfort by carrying their earrings in their pockets to parties and balls and assuming the ornaments on arrival, padding the backs of the lobes with small pieces of silk.

Fashionable women inevitably suffered permanent distension of the earlobes, which were dragged down by the weight of the girandoles. This fate did not prevent their descendants from participating in another fashion for huge earrings in the late 1820s and 1830s and suffering the same consequences. One of the most enthusiastic young adherents of the vogue was the future Queen Victoria, who often wore her grandmother Queen Charlotte's girandole earrings of 1761. Photographs of Queen Victoria in old age, when she sometimes took to simple single-stone or pearl earrings, show them lodged on elongated earlobes. Fortunately the huge variety of new types and fittings means that no one now has to wear one kind of earring for a prolonged period.

Shirley Bury

Authors' note

This book has been written for a number of reasons. Firstly, earrings have been the most desired item of jewellery over the past decade; most women possess many and without them they feel naked. Secondly, unlike other items of jewellery, earrings have evolved dramatically in shape, size and design since their origins in 3000 BC. Thirdly, earrings are unique in Western jewellery, penetrating the body and assuming identity with aural acupuncture. And lastly, we have both been worshippers and wearers of earrings and wish to share our fascination. The scope of the subject has unfortunately required us to limit this book to mainstream earrings of Western women. We have had to exclude the development of male and ethnic earrings and to some extent 20th-century designer jewellers.

Daniela Mascetti
Amanda Triossi

1

The historical background:
from antiquity
to the 17th century

The earliest archaeological evidence for earrings dates from the 3rd millennium BC, but it seems likely that men and women will have adorned their ears with, for example, shells and polished pebbles for centuries before that.

The idea of piercing the earlobe to insert a metallic ornament originated in the Orient. From the start earrings can be divided into two types: the simple rigid hoop in its numerous variations, and the more elaborate articulated pendant. In Antiquity, they were amongst the most popular means of personal ornament.

Around 2500 BC Sumerian women were adorning their ears with gold earrings in the form of single or double crescents, as revealed by findings in the royal graves of Ur in what is now Iraq. The crescent form, comprising two thin sheets of gold soldered together with a hollowed centre, was a simple yet successful design which was to spread towards the West and remains to this day a favourite shape of earring. More elaborate Babylonian examples of the early 2nd millennium BC, also from Ur, show how the simple crescent motif could be embellished with embossed decoration, the details picked out with filigree and granulation.

Minoan and Mycenean

Early examples of earrings with a tapered hoop design, in a way a thinner version of the crescent- or boat-shaped earring, have been found in graves in Anatolia and Greece. Hooped earrings of gold, silver and bronze, tapered at the ends, have also been excavated in Crete and date from the Middle Minoan period (2000–1600 BC). p. 25

It is not until the second half of the 2nd millennium BC that we find variations and elaborations of the crescent or hoop type; during the Late Minoan and Early Mycenean period (1600–1100 BC) earrings in the form of scalloped or tapered hoops were common in Mycaene, while in Crete during the same period the most widespread form of earring consisted of a tapered hoop decorated with a conical pendant representing a clear progression from the earlier simple hoop.

The tapered hoop supporting a conical pendant was also popular in Cyprus, where several examples come from 13th and 12th century BC graves in Enkomi. Judging from the number of extant examples, this type had a long life; a less elaborate version consisting of a tapered hoop supporting a smaller bead cluster is well testified both in Crete and in Cyprus; it may have been cast in one piece, as a steatite mould of this shape has been found in Crete. This type continued in Cyprus throughout the Dark Ages, reappearing amongst Greek designs of the 7th century BC.

By the end of the 2nd millennium BC, the hoop earring, tapering to a different degree at each end, was widely dispersed in the Aegean world, Western Asia, Cyprus and Syria, as revealed by many excavations.

In Cyprus, from the middle of the 2nd millennium BC, and particularly during the third quarter, earrings were very popular and may have had some supernatural significance, since contemporary painted terracotta idols in the form of stylized nude females, probably fertility symbols, have their earlobes pierced two or three times and large terracotta hoops suspended from them.

The simple, tapered hoop was worn there from about 1400 BC, where it arrived possibly from Crete but more likely from Syria; it continued in Cyprus for a long time, surviving throughout the Dark Ages, and was reintroduced from there into Greece around the 7th century BC.

A variation of this type, of either Cypriot or Syrian invention, consists of a hoop of twisted or plaited gold wire. Also to be found is the 'leech' earring, a sort of elongated tapered hoop, the lower part expanded into a fat crescent motif. Hoops supporting clusters of beads or elongated conical pendants decorated with granulation were, as we have already seen, as popular in Crete as they were in Cyprus. A typical Cypriot earring of the 13th century BC was a hoop supporting a bull's head pendant stamped out of thin sheet gold. Although the shape of the pendant is a common Mycenean motif, no contemporary examples have been found on the Greek mainland.

When, in about 1100 BC, the Mycenean world succumbed to the Achaean invasion, which was followed by the three centuries of poverty and near-barbarism known as the Dark Ages, the arts declined and jewellery in precious metal became rare. It is likely that the main sources of gold at the time were the tombs of earlier periods. Among the limited number of gold ornaments such as finger-rings, bracelets, pins and fibulae, there survived a small number of spirals, the purpose of which is still not certain, but which may have been earrings or hair-ornaments.

The brilliant civilization of Cyprus was destroyed at the same time, but traditions lived on and the Achaeans left intact the long-established Mycenean techniques. Goldsmiths worked throughout the Dark Ages preserving and perpetuating forms and designs that were to be reintroduced into Greece around the 7th century BC.

Egypt

In Ancient Egypt jewels were an important part of costume; they were worn by men and children as well as by women, and were often used to adorn statues of gods and goddesses. Images of sacred animals such as cats and crocodiles are often given necklaces, bracelets and earrings made of gold. Earrings, introduced from Asia, seem to have appeared later than other types of jewellery and the earliest important example dates from the end of the second intermediary period (circa 1600 BC). This is a pair consisting of several hoops soldered together which would have hung from large holes pierced in the earlobes. Another early type is a simple hoop of gold, glass paste, faience, jasper or other semiprecious stone worn by pulling the earlobe through the open end, something that was possibly done in infancy.

X-ray photographs of mummies in the Cairo Museum show earlobes extremely elongated and deformed by the use of very heavy ear ornaments in childhood. One mummy in the museum of Turin has two earrings worn on the same earlobe. The mummy of Tutankhamen has large holes pierced in the earlobes, proving that earrings were worn by men as well as women.

During the New Kingdom (1559–1085 BC) large earplugs came into fashion and these also caused deformation of the earlobes. They are designed as faience discs and have a groove round the edge which enabled them to fit into an enlarged hole stretched in the earlobes. Other ear ornaments of contemporary date were in the form of mushroom-shaped studs with the stem pushed through such a hole. In both cases these ornaments were worn in the plane of the ear rather than at right angles to it.

By the end of the XVIIIth Dynasty the decoration of earrings was very varied: cascades of drops, flowers and bell-shaped motifs for pendent earrings and rosettes and p. 26, 27 flowerhead motifs for the large discs.

The Greek World

Around 800 BC contacts between Greece and the East became closer and two centuries of Oriental influence in Greek art followed. Cyprus and Syria – taken in the broad sense to include Phoenicia and the Neo-Hittite North Syria – were the two countries that mainly influenced Greece, the latter acting as a channel for Egyptian and Mesopotamian influence.

The relative abundance of gold artefacts of this period is undoubtedly related to the opening up of the East to the Greek world through colonization, giving access to rich sources of precious metal in Asia Minor, especially to the Lydian gold mines. The preponderance of the ateliers of Eastern Greece throughout the period is evidence of this. Embossing, filigree and granulation grew in popularity and inlaying with stones, amber and glass made its appearance. Gold earrings of flat crescent design, often decorated with granulation and inlays, and suspended with fine chains are well represented, as well as earrings designed as spirals to be thrust through a hole in the lobe. They were either simple gold wire spirals or had a variety of finials decorated with beading and granulation, worn with the ends pointing upwards. Many variations of this type are known, some with more, some with fewer turns of thin and thick gold wire, others splayed out in the form of a letter W with a higher central point. In the late 7th century the W-shaped spiral was sometimes decorated with elaborate finials in the shape of griffins' heads, pomegranates or rams heads of Oriental inspiration.

The crescent or boat-shaped earring of Eastern tradition, seen in Ur in the middle of the 3rd millennium BC, finally reached Greece via Syria and Cyprus about 700 BC and the type was to flourish there and in the Hellenized centres of the Eastern Mediterranean for some four centuries. Greek examples of the 7th century BC are characterized by a rather fat boat-shaped motif, sometimes decorated with granulation, on a thin gold wire going through the pierced earlobe. The hoop with beaded pendant of Cypriot tradition became popular in the 7th and 6th centuries BC but remained confined to Eastern Greece.

Greek jewellery of the 6th and early 5th centuries is of artistic brilliance but very little has survived. It is, however, amply documented in vase painting and sculpture. Three of the few regions relatively rich in archaic gold jewellery are Sicily, Rhodes and Cyprus, where crescent earrings of the traditional form continued to be produced.

It was not until after the Persian wars that gold became more plentiful in Greece. By the accidents of history, this Greek Classical jewellery is better known from examples found in Southern Russia, Cyprus and Southern Italy than from Greece proper. The forms were extremely varied and among the abundance of diadems, necklaces, bracelets, pendants and finger-rings, earrings were very popular. They came in three main forms: the boat or crescent, the spiral or helix, and the disc with cone or inverted pyramid pendant.

As in the Archaic period, vase painting and sculpture would seem to suggest that earrings were the most popular form of ornament; statues of female figures were frequently adorned with them, sometimes sculpted in marble and sometimes made of precious metal, as can be inferred from the holes pierced in the ears. It is possible that the ornaments created to adorn statues or donated to temples to be worn by images of goddesses in religious processions were more elaborate, rich and complex than those used in ordinary life, which were buried with the dead and have now been recovered from graves. That they were part of ordinary dress is proved by representation on coins, vase paintings and terracotta figures.

As already mentioned, most of these surviving examples came from areas outside mainland Greece, such as Etruria and Southern Italy.

The boat-shaped earring, which, as we have seen, dates back at least to 13th-century Cyprus, was the most popular form of ear ornament in the Classical period. In its simplest form it consisted of a crescent terminating in a wire for insertion into the earlobe, and remained in fashion, virtually without a break, throughout antiquity. In the 5th and 4th centuries BC it was widespread throughout Southern Russia, Thracia, Macedonia and also Sicily where it was depicted on Syracusan coins of 474–450 BC adorning the head of Artemis-Arethusa.

p. 25 The earliest examples from the Classical period are very simple, consisting of a boat-shaped motif decorated with beading, filigree and granulation. Later, in the second half of the 4th century BC, they tend to be more elaborate in design, often with suspended pendants and chains of various types. Among the most complex examples of the boat-shaped earring is one from Tarentum where the boat is completely encrusted with filigree, granulation, leaf and palmette motifs and is merely a vehicle p. 27 for the exuberant decoration of rosettes, nikai, doves, chains and pendants. This decorative repertoire of palmettes, rosettes, flowerheads and spirals can also be found, enlarged, on contemporary vase painting and funerary monuments. The Tarentum example perfectly illustrates the general trend of the period towards increasing elaboration of decoration which is common to the whole Hellenic world. The heavy use of filigree floral motifs and stylized palmettes to enliven the flat surface of the basic boat-shape and the curved surface of the rosette petals are deliberately intended to create a complex chiaroscuro effect with light, shade and reflection and give drama and depth to the object; in later periods this effect was often achieved chromatically by the combination of various different gemstones and by the use of multicoloured enamels.

It is interesting to note that even at this stage the craftsmen of Tarentum were also catering for a less prosperous clientèle, making gilt terracotta imitations of the type described above, probably cast in moulds taken from the more expensive gold examples – although it is possible that these cheaper, rather fragile ornaments were made specifically as grave goods.

Another very popular form of earring of the second half of the 5th century BC was that in the form of a disc supporting either one or three pendants, the central one invariably being a female head, an inverted pyramid, an amphora or a cone and the two flanking ones articulated chains with links of various types. By the Hellenistic period disc-and-pendant earrings were to become the most popular and widespread form of ear ornament.

Among the earliest examples is a superb pair from Tarentum, each with a disc dec- p. 27 orated at the centre with a filigree rosette within a border of corded wire and beaded work and a female head suspended from a central pendant flanked by two chains of conical beads with bell-shaped terminals. The female head pendants are chased in great detail, with the hairstyle typical of the time as seen on terracottas, vase paintings and coins: parted at the centre, divided in two bandeaux and gathered in a large bun worn low on the nape of the neck. The hair being brushed away from the ears leaves ample space for a large pair of earrings consisting of a pyramidal cluster of beads suspended from a rosette. The great popularitiy of earrings throughout antiquity is certainly linked to the fashion for women to wear the hair gathered at the top or the back of the head, or at least brushed away from the temples.

The head-shaped pendants show an interesting feature: at the base there is a small hole into which it is likely that a piece of sponge or cloth soaked in perfumed oil was inserted. Putting perfumed sponges in necklace pendants was common in antiquity, and Etruscan earrings with perfume compartments have been found. Though not common, such earrings with female head pendants have been recovered in Southern Russia, Cyprus and Etruria.

Another highly significant detail on this example is the presence on the disc and chains of small traces of delicately coloured enamel. The introduction of polychrome enamels in jewellery was an important innovation that dramatically transformed the work of Greek goldsmiths, who had until then achieved effects of movement and contrast through the use of filigree and granulation. It is unfortunate that in this and many other examples the major part of the enamel has now worn away, since polychrome enamels defined the different elements of the decoration, and were therefore essential to the overall effect of the piece.

Rather more widely dispersed were disc earrings with an inverted pyramid pendant often between two chains. This type of pendant, already seen in the Archaic and early Classical periods, became very fashionable towards the end of the 5th century, reaching the height of its popularity in the 4th century BC, and continued to be one of the favourite forms of ear ornament of the Hellenistic period: many examples have been found in Cyprus, Southern Russia, Macedonia and Apulia. The type is also represented on coins from Elis, Locri, Metapontum and Tarentum, on the *tetradrachm* of Eukleidas from Syracuse, and on 4th-century BC terracotta antefixes from Tarentum, Metapontum and Heraclea.

The earliest examples are characterized by extremely elaborate gold leaf applications, filigree and granulation on both disc and pyramidal pendant. Later examples are simpler and often completely undecorated apart from a gemstone, usually a garnet, set at the centre of the disc. Gemstones, which made their first appearance in jewellery towards the end of the 4th century BC, became more and more prominent from now until Roman times.

p. 26

Contemporary with the earring types described above and just as important were disc earrings with a vase or a cone pendant. They enjoyed a long period of popularity, peaking between the 2nd and 1st century BC. Tarentum, Cyprus and Southern Russia offer the best examples, often set with garnets, coloured glass beads and pearls. This type is well documented on Syracusan and African coins of the 3rd and 2nd century BC.

28, 29

Hellenistic art is cosmopolitan in character, the same forms being found all over the Eastern Mediterranean. Jewellery was no exception; examples from Apulia are hardly distinguishable from those from Thessaly, Macedonia, Asia Minor, Thrace or Southern Russia.

p. 31

Particularly popular in the 2nd century BC were disc earrings with bird pendants made of glass paste. Sirens, peacocks and other winged creatures naturalistically modelled in this way were widely popular. The dove was a special favourite because of its assocation with Aphrodite.

25, 26, 27

Another variation on the same theme is where the pendant assumes the shape of a miniature Eros. Eros, tutelary god of death and love with his double symbolism, erotic and funerary, is a very common motif in Hellenistic jewellery from the late 4th to the late 2nd century BC and is represented in various ways. Almost as popular was Nike or Victory, a feminine version of Eros. With time, emphasis on the human figure became so pronounced that the disc disappeared, leaving Eros or Nike simply suspended from the earlobe by means of a hook of gold wire.

Another very popular type of ear ornament from the Classical period is the helix earring, comprising a tubular piece of thin gold leaf twisted into a spiral with various decorative motifs as terminals. This had already existed in the Archaic period and was very well known to the Oriental Greek world as early as the 7th century BC. Many examples have been found in Cyprus, Rhodes, Thrace, Macedonia and Southern

Russia, all related to the same prototype, probably of Cypriot origin, descended from the Mycenean spirals of Enkomi. Towards the mid-4th century BC, another form of earring appeared, consisting of an open circle with a small pointed finial on one side and a larger terminal in the shape of a human or animal head on the other. There are similar examples with human or animal heads on both terminals, one larger than the other. These remained popular throughout the Hellenized world until the beginning of the 1st century BC. The favourite motif for the terminal was the lion head, but antelopes', rams', dogs' and bulls' heads are also known, their eyes set with gemstones or coloured glass pastes.

Both helix and animals' head earrings raise the question of how they were worn. By modern standards they seem too large to be pushed through a hole in the earlobe, but no alternative fitting has ever been found. We must assume, therefore, that in the past women submitted themselves to far greater tortures than we are prepared to suffer today for the sake of fashion.

The conquests of Alexander the Great between 333 and 322 BC transformed the Greek world. Vast territories came within the Greek sphere of influence, while at the same time Greece itself was exposed to influences from Egypt and Asia. The Hellenistic age, as culturally and artistically defined, lasted from about 322 BC until the inauguration of the Roman Empire in 27 BC. Much jewellery has survived from this period. Gold became more widely available through intensive mining in Thrace and the dispersal of captured Persian treasures.

Earrings were designed as simple gold hoops either decorated at the front with a single motif, such as a bird, a dolphin, a bunch of grapes, or a negro's head, or having a pendant in the form of such a motif. Much use was made of glass paste and gemstones to pick out details and create contrasts of colour, and a new technique known as 'dipped enamel' was introduced to give a multicoloured effect, especially to earring pendants in the shape of birds or other creatures. p. 26,

Together with these types, which are very typical of their period, many other earrings of older design continued to be produced and amongst these the disc-and-pendant model was perhaps the favourite.

Etruscan
The earliest remains of the Etruscans of central Italy are dated about 700 BC, continuing in a recognizable form until about the 1st century BC. Their great wealth, attributable largely to the mineral resources of the country, is reflected in the sumptuousness of their tombs. In female graves, vessels of precious metal and silver and gold jewellery such as fibulae, pectorals, bracelets and elaborate earrings reflect not only the important role women had in that society, but also jewellery's function of 'hoard' and 'reserve fund'. Although in its earliest manifestations Etruscan art was remarkably free of Greek influences, it did not long remain so, and by the end of the

7th century BC Greek artistic influence was becoming increasingly significant. Etruscan art, however, never lost its identity completely.

The earliest Etruscan earrings, of about 625 BC, in the shape of crescents and hoops, are not dissimilar to those found elsewhere in the Greek world at the same time. The first truly Etruscan form of earring made its appearance just before the mid-6th century. The type is known as a *baule*, Italian for a bag or a travelling case, and it is perhaps the best known form of Etruscan ornament. Its popularity lasted just over a century. It consists of a strip of gold leaf bent round to form a cylinder, the two ends connected by a gold wire also acting as a suspension hoop. The ends of the cylinder were sometimes closed by a circular gold plate. The decoration, consisting of gold leaf application in the form of stylized flowers and rosettes, embossed leaves or geometrical motifs, filigree and granulation occasionally embellished with polychrome enamels, shows a certain 'horror vacui', pressing as many decorative details as possible onto the small gold surface.

Another type of earring of typical Etruscan design, which first appeared in the second half of the 6th century, is the disc richly decorated with concentric bands of floral and geometrical motifs embossed or made of filigree and granulation, often inlayed with gemstones, amber or glass paste. Earstuds would perhaps be a more appropriate name for this type of ornament, with a hollow tube at the back ending in a loop to be pushed through the earlobe and a safety chain attached to the side of the disc for fixing the loop. The origin of these large ear-ornaments, which in some cases measure as much as 7cms in diameter, is probably Lydia.

In the 5th century BC the most fashionable and widespread form of ornament in the Etruscan world was a type of earring consisting of a tubular hoop decorated at one end with the head of a woman, a river-god, a ram or a lion. With slight variations, it remained popular throughout the 4th and 3rd centuries BC.

Among the most characteristic earrings of the 4th and 3rd centuries is the horseshoe-shaped plaque type, mounted with a cluster of embossed globules, hollow inside in order to act as containers for perfumed oil. An entirely Etruscan creation, these earrings were very popular throughout the country as can be seen from the many surviving examples and their frequent reproduction on terracotta and vase paintings. Particularly interesting in this respect is a group of votive statues found in Lavinium, depicting female figures bejewelled with necklaces and earrings of this type apparently moulded directly from the gold originals. These cluster earrings remain very frequent in tombs of the 4th century BC and tend to disappear in favour of new models coming from abroad only towards the end of the Classical age.

What we can describe as a 'Greek Taste' did not appear in Etruscan jewellery until the last thirty years of the 4th century and must be seen in the context of the general process of Hellenization which followed the conquests of Alexander the Great. The typical Etruscan forms gradually disappeared to be replaced by the more international disc-and-pendants, the pendants supporting shapes such as inverted

. 28, 29

p. 31

p. 30

29, 31

pyramids, birds, bells and amphorae, or by hoops decorated at the front with amber heads of negroes. In some examples local tradition and external influence blend together; e.g., a gold hoop, decorated at the front with a horseshoe-shaped motif typical of the Etruscan taste, supporting a female head pendant of pure Tarentine inspiration.

p. 34,

Rome and Byzantium

Examples of silver and gold jewellery from pre-Republican and Republican Rome are very scarce. From those that survive we can conclude that between 700 and 250 BC Roman jewellery was for all practical purposes Etruscan. Material is even scarcer for the period between 250 and 27 BC, but we may assume that Roman jewellery, as well as Etruscan, was basically the same as Hellenistic.

For many centuries jewellery was a luxury looked upon with official disapproval in the Roman world. The amounts of gold which might be buried with the dead and which a Roman lady might wear were fixed by law. Certain items of personal adornment, moreover, such as finger rings, were strictly reserved to certain social classes and for specific occasions.

By 27 BC, when the Roman empire was established, Rome had finally swallowed up the remnants of the Hellenistic world with the annexation of Egypt in 30 BC. The political changes, however, had very little effect on minor arts, and during the first years of the empire jewellery continued to be produced in Hellenistic forms. The major centres of jewellery manufacture were the old Hellenistic centres of Antioch and Alexandria, followed by Rome itself. Progressively wealth, luxury and ostentation replaced Republican sobriety and jewellery became important in display.

In the eastern part of the empire and in Egypt earrings designed as plain hoops or hoops decorated with human and animal heads of Hellenistic tradition continued to be produced with only minor variations until the 2nd century AD. Other types consisted of long S-shaped hooks with variously designed pendants. A new type appeared suddenly in the 1st century AD and lasted for about a hundred years. It consisted of a gold hemisphere with an S-shaped hook fitted at the back, sometimes surmounted by a similar but smaller boss. This was very popular: many examples have been found as far apart as Rome, Cyprus, Siphnos and Palestine, and it is also frequently depicted on mummy portraits. Closely related is a type consisting of a spherical cluster of pearls or beads.

p. 32
p. 25

In the course of the 2nd century AD a whole new class of earrings appeared, quite unrelated to Hellenistic shapes. In its simplest form it consisted of a gemstone set in a large bezel holding a drop pendant, secured to the earlobe by means of an S-shaped hook. During the same period earrings were produced in the form of circular gem-set elements supporting horizontal bars with two or three pendants. Gemstones including sapphires, emeralds, aquamarines and topazes were by now freely employed in jewellery.

Literary sources such as Pliny, Seneca and Petronius have much to say on the subject of *inaures* and *pendentes*. Earrings were the favourite manner of displaying wealth for the patrician lady who often turned for advice to the *auricolae ornatrices*, women whose job was to attend to the problems caused by prolonged wearing of large and heavy earrings. The new extravagance has been referred to by Pliny who tells us that Caligula's wife Lollia Paulina wore emeralds and pearls on her hair, head, arms and fingers as well as on her ears at everyday functions. Women, he says, liked to wear earrings set with two or three pearl drops that rattled at the slightest movement of the head; hence their name of *crotalia*.

During the 3rd century AD the Roman empire began to crumble; during the 4th it was divided into an eastern and a western empire; and during the 5th the western half collapsed leaving only the eastern empire, governed from Constantinople (formerly Byzantium). One effect of these changes was that Oriental influences were again powerful in Western art, but as far as jewellery is concerned, Roman techniques and forms continued to be used and earrings with two or three gemset pendent drops remained normal.

32, 33

Earrings appeared to have fallen from favour during the Byzantine period, with fashionable ladies preferring to wear large and elaborate ornaments on the temple or sides of the face, similar to those worn by the empress Theodora in the mosaic of San Vitale in Ravenna, but they did not completely disappear. The only truly Byzantine form of earring which was popular in the late 6th and 7th centuries consists of a large but light pierced gold crescent decorated with openwork stylized flower and scroll motifs.

In western Europe, jewellery production declined drastically, and only one form of earring stands out as original. This consists of a wire hoop, simple or twisted, decorated with a polyhedral motif, usually inset with garnets. The popularity of this type is confirmed by finds from Ostrogothic, Merovingian and Southern Russian sites dating from the 5th to the 9th century.

The Middle Ages

Although the Middle Ages and the Renaissance are particularly rich periods for jewellery in general, the role of earrings is so minor that one can say that they virtually disappear for the six hundred years between the 11th and 16th centuries. The reason for this is to be found in hair and dress fashion: elaborate hairstyles, head-dresses and high collared costumes left very little scope for earrings.

In the Middle Ages it was customary for a woman, especially married women, to conceal their hair with a coiffe *hubet* and from the middle of the 12th century with a *barbette*, which consisted of a stiffened head-band worn with a chin strap concealing the ears. Respectable married women had to keep their heads covered when seen in public, a rule which went back to St Paul: 'For if the woman be not covered, let her be shorn or shaven: if it be a shame for a woman to be shorn or shaven let her be covered.' The concealment of a woman's hair was a way of demonstrating dependency on her husband who was the only man with the privilege of seeing it (a woman loosening her *barbette* in public would be regarded as unladylike and morally lax) and explains why unmarried girls were allowed to wear long and flowing hair. In both cases, however, the scope for earrings was non-existent; with the *barbette* the chin band covered the ears and the cheeks, not only preventing the use of earrings but also hindering eating and even speaking; on the other hand unmarried girls with their hair flowing over their ears also did not have the opportunity to display earrings. During the 13th century written evidence for earrings occurs only in books like the *Roman de la Rose* where unusual jewels such as earrings are listed: 'Et met a ses deux oreilletes. Deus verges d'or pendans greletes'.

Around the middle of the 14th century hair fashions underwent a considerable change, becoming much more elaborate and frequently embellished with precious head ornaments. One of the typical coiffures, which developed at the end of the 14th p. 37 century and retained its popularity for more than a hundred years, consisted of two thick braids of hair looped over the ears; another consisted of hair puffed out and padded over the ears and kept in shape by a gold net. The changes, however, did not improve the scope for earrings.

The Renaissance
During the 15th century in northern Europe the fashion for very elaborate and complex head coverings continued: the voluminous double horned headdress was extremely popular as well as the sugarloaf headdress *hennine*. In early Renaissance Italy this fashion subsided and the natural beauty of the hair was appreciated once more. This did not mean that very elaborate coiffures were not devised to enhance that beauty. Indeed a popular type of hair arrangement consisted of the hair drawn up into a chignon at the back with a wide band, a ribbon or a strand of pearls known as *frenello* encircling the head and usually decorated at the centre with a jewel in the form of a flowerhead cluster. With such an abundance of jewels on the head and with the ears concealed beneath the head-band, there was still no point in wearing earrings. This can clearly be seen in the portrait of Battista Sforza (circa 1465) by Piero della p. 36 Francesca, in which the Duchess displays a great number of jewels on her head, one fastened to the band at the top and three smaller clusters securing the very elaborate coil of hair placed over the ears. Also popular were rich be-jewelled hairnets placed at the back of the head with the hair combed over the ears and the stones set amongst the gold threads. An inventory of the jewels of Ippolita Sforza given to her on the occasion of her marriage to Alfonso of Aragon in 1465 mentions a net set with 89 rubies and 464 pearls. There was, therefore, no place for earrings. Even when no head jewels were worn the hair was left hanging down in curls over the ears. Throughout the 15th century in Italy, earrings are never mentioned in inventories.

After centuries of neglect, earrings begin to make a timid appearance in Italy around the 1530s, mainly prompted by a change in fashion in hairstyles in favour of parting the hair at the centre and drawing it away from the face which was framed by a padded roll. The design of the new earrings was fairly simple: usually a plain gold hoop with a single pearl drop. This type of earring is depicted frequently in contemporary portraiture but hardly any examples survive. This is because pearls are one of the few organic materials employed in jewellery, and, unlike gemstones, they only last about 300 years.

Another design for which there is pictorial evidence can be seen in a portrait, by Moroni of the mid-to-late 1550s in the National Gallery, London. It shows a pearl drop suspended from a gold spherical element and connected to the gold hoop in the ear by a satin ribbon bow matching the colour of the dress. This is one of the earliest records of this kind of earring, but the combination of satin or velvet ribbon bows and jewelled elements becomes a recurring feature in early and mid-17th century earrings. All earrings were worn with pierced ears: a hoop was threaded through the ear to support the pendent element. The screw and clip fitting is a comparatively recent innovation apparently unknown during the Renaissance. The single mention of the clip earrings which occurs in Cellini's autobiography merely proves that they were not in common use: Cellini describes dressing up a friend to impersonate a woman at a party given by Michelangelo: 'In his ears I placed two little rings, set with two large and fair pearls: the rings were broken; they only clipped his ears as though they had been pierced.'

In other parts of Europe, and especially the north, earrings remained out of fashion, the reason again being that elaborate headdresses such as the horseshoe bonnet went on the back of the head and down over the ears.

Towards the end of the 16th century the use of pendent earrings was still limited p. 36 not so much now by headgear but by the new fashion for very high and stiff ruff collars. The extreme examples of the high ruff occur in Spain, England and France, and in these countries women continued to be unable to wear earrings for about one hundred years after their reintroduction in Italy. They are seldom seen in portraits and are not mentioned in contemporary inventories such as those of the jewels of the French crown from François I to Henri III; grand parures of jewels are repeatedly referred to but these include not earrings but items known as 'bordures d'oreilletes', a jewelled ornament that encircles the head from one ear to the other. The only mention of earrings comes in the *Chronique du Bourgeois de Paris*, in a descripton of the jewels worn by Eleonore of Austria at her arrival in France for her marriage with François I in 1529: 'hanging from her ears were two large stones as big as nuts'. The earrings were part of the jewellery which she had brought from Spain, and reflect a southern European fashion. In fact her fondness for large, Spanish style earrings is displayed in a portrait where she wears large elliptical gold ones set with three pearls supporting a fringe of a further three pearls.

Shortly before 1600 the high ruff collar gave way to the standing collar, freeing the area around the neck, and long pendent earrings finally began to make their appearance in northern Europe. They are clearly visible in the portrait of Queen Anne of Denmark painted by De Critz at the beginning of the 17th century – large baroque pearls linked by gold-set lozenge-shaped diamonds to gold suspension loops which are completely concealed by red ribbon bows. Two features are noteworthy: the use of the ribbon bows, which had already appeared half a century before in Italy and continued to be favoured in the first half of the 17th century; and the use of large faceted diamonds. It was around this time that improved techniques of gem-cutting prompted a shift in emphasis from the gold and enamel setting typical of Renaissance jewellery to the faceted gemstone.

p. 36
p. 38

The 17th Century

As earrings began to gain independence at the beginning of the 17th century a variety of new designs made their appearance, exemplified by those of Arnold Lulls, a Netherlands-born jeweller (active in England circa 1585–circa 1621) greatly favoured by James I of England and his consort Anne of Denmark. Prominent among them were aigrettes (a plume-shaped ornament) and earrings set with faceted gemstones. His book of coloured drawings includes three pages of designs for earrings; one page shows two different pairs of earrings. The first has three green pear-shaped stones, the largest at the centre, suspended from a gold crescent enamelled in white and set with a step-cut ruby; the green enamel suspension loop is in the form of a serpent with four square-cut diamonds set on its head. The second pair is similar but has only one drop, the central element being set with faceted diamonds and the hoop with rubies. Another page shows a pair of earrings, each formed from two pear-shaped pearls with a larger green gemstone suspended from an openwork surmount set with eleven table-cut diamonds. It is worth pointing out that at this time all diamonds portrayed in designs and paintings were painted black, the reason being that diamonds were set in closed settings backed by a black foil or varnish and therefore would appear, in reality, nearly black.

p. 38, 39

By the early 1600s designs were already fairly elaborate compared to the plain pearl drops which had been common up to then: noteworthy is the serpent-shaped hoop and the use of faceted gemstones reflecting the new interest in cut stones and especially diamonds in consequence of the improved techniques of cutting. Also new is the use of the three drops which will remain a favourite form of earring for two centuries. It most probably derives from the three pearl drops, a larger one in the middle flanked by two smaller, always found suspended from Renaissance pendants. It is interesting that in early 17th-century earrings all elements remain very separate: the hoop, the central element and the drop, and it is only at the end of the century that all parts of earrings begin to be conceived of as a whole. Besides conventional earrings, the rather bizarre fashion for earstrings developed in Britain around 1620. These were suspended not from the ear but from a cord at the sides of the face or a loose corkscrew of hair.

The popularity of earrings at the turn of the 17th century is clear from an inventory of the personal items of Catherine de Médicis, Queen of France, compiled in 1610, which lists nine pairs of earrings all set with faceted diamonds and gemstones.

One of the best collections of this period is the Cheapside Hoard, now in the Museum of London and the British Museum, part of a jeweller's stock, probably hidden in London about 1640 because of the English Civil War. It includes an elaborate pendent earring in the form of three white enamel links supporting ten amethyst briolettes; the suspension loop is missing. Again evident is the interest in cut stone and in a complex design.

During the second quarter of the 17th century there was a change in favour of greater simplicity in dress and ornament, but this seems not to have disturbed the newly established popularity of earrings. Very large pearl drops were one of the favourite types. The difficulty of finding two beautiful pearls matched in size, shape and colour made these earrings extremely valuable and sought after; they were known as 'union d'excellence' earrings, the large pear-shaped pearls emerging from flowing curls. At times it is one large pearl, at others one may find two or three pearls hanging from one ear, as can be seen in the English portrait of Ann Carr, Countess of Bedford, painted by Anthony Van Dyck (1599–1644). The fact that so few of these examples have survived is partly because they have decayed and partly because pearls can easily be mounted in a new setting and, unlike a faceted gemstone, are not easy to identify. Only one exceptional pair of pearl earrings still exists today, though not in their original 17th-century setting. They are two extremely large natural pear-shaped pearls known as the Marie Mancini pearls; they were given by Louis XIV to his mistress Marie Mancini, niece of Cardinal Mazarin.

P. 37

The importance attached to pearl earrings is also substantiated by contemporary literature: Francis de Sales, in his *Introduction à la vie devote* of 1608 which was reprinted (mainly in Antwerp) thirteen times in the 17th century alone, writes in a chapter entitled 'Advice to the Married' that:

> Women of both ancient and present times customarily hang pearls from their ears because of the pleasure they derive (as Pliny observes) from feeling them swing when they touch each other. But because I know that God's great friend, Isaac, sent earrings as the first token of his love to the pure Rebecca, so do I believe that this jewel signifies spirituality; that the first part that a man must have from his wife and which the wife must faithfully preserve is the ear, so that no speech or sound may enter in other than the sweet sound of chaste words which are oriental pearls of the Gospel.

The expression 'pearls of the Gospel' derives from the parable of the merchant searching for rare pearls in Matthew 13 and is used by Sales as a metaphor for Christ's teachings.

Around the middle of the 17th century earrings had become an essential item of adornment and their shapes were becoming increasingly complex and interesting. It is known that Louis XIV gave an important pair of emerald and diamond earrings to his mistress Madame de Soubise, who used them to signal to the king that her husband had left Paris and that they were free to meet. Typical of the new complexity of design is a pair of polychrome enamel turquoise and ruby earrings designed as an openwork garland of floral motifs carrying a fringe of pearls, the centre decorated with a tulip, and suspended on a flowerhead cluster surmount. As well as the overall intricacy, it is interesting to notice how the contemporary interest in flowers, especially tulips, is reflected in these earrings. At the end of the 16th century a garden with hothouses in Paris had plants which served as models for designers of embroidery; later the establishment was bought by Henri IV and the Jardin du Roi, as it was then called, remained a centre for the study of rare and beautiful flowers. But it was the increased European contacts with the Levant that brought exotic flowers to the forefront, and the tulip, first seen in the West in 1559, conquered Europe; in 1634 it generated a real tulip 'rage' known as tulipomania. This explains why tulip motifs are to occur so prominently on contemporary jewels. On one pair of pendent earrings the front is typically set with faceted gemstones, rubies and emeralds supporting a fringe of pearls; but the back is decorated with three tulip flowerheads in painted black and red enamel on a light blue enamel ground.

p. 40

Around 1660 the girandole, which became a very successful form of earring, emerged. It consisted of two main elements worked into a coherent design: a stylized ribbon bow surmount supporting three pear-shaped drops. The bow motif undoubtedly derives from the ribbon bow used in earlier earrings made of satin or velvet in a colour to match the dress; the three drops derive from early 17th-century examples, such as those of Arnold Lulls, going back ultimately to the three pearl drops suspended from Renaissance brooches. The girandole is an extremely becoming shape of earring, as it fills out the space around the ear to complement the face. Its popularity is attested by numerous engravings of the 1660s, such as those by Gilles Légaré and François Lefebvre. The engraved designs frequently show front and back views of the girandole; the front was set either entirely with faceted gemstones or with three pear-shaped pearls; the back was decorated with enamelwork, a feature that distinguished the early girandoles from later examples. Frequently the designs for the girandole earrings are accompanied by those of brooches of similar design known as sévignés which would have been worn together as a set. Drawings which record the earrings owned by Anne of Austria, the wife of Louis XIII, show girandoles of great elegance set with diamonds of exceptional dimensions; while the inventory of the jewels of Marie Thérèse, the wife of Louis XIV, dated 1691, lists various girandoles: two pairs set with diamonds, one with very rare stones, the other with pearls.

p. 57

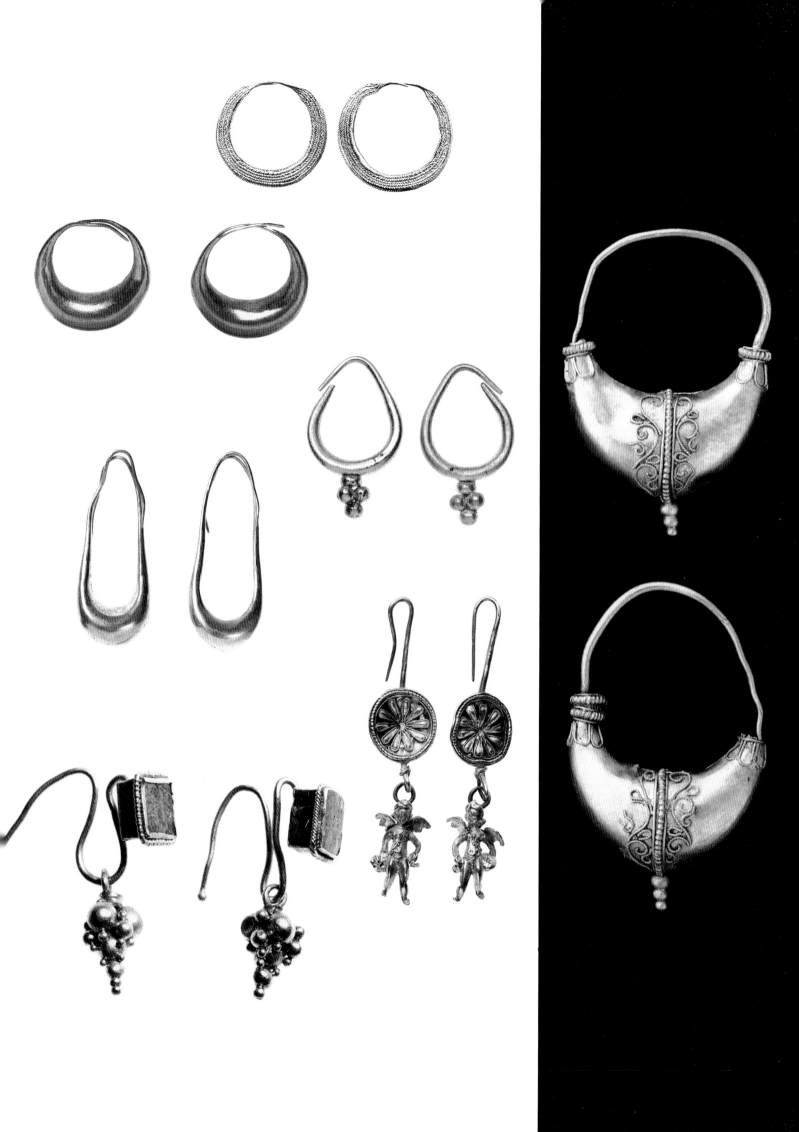

FASHIONS IN THE ANCIENT WORLD

Right: Part of a wall-painting from Thebes, New Kingdom, circa 1400 BC, depicting a scene from a banquet. Three Egyptian beauties are wearing the large earrings or earplugs fashionable at the time. Designed as faience or gold discs, they had a groove round the edge which fitted into a hole in the earlobe.

Below from left to right:
A pair of gold, enamel and glass paste earrings designed as a bunch of grapes suspended from a vine leaf, Canosa, late 3rd/early 2nd century BC. The fragments of green enamel on the leaves and the purple-red glass paste beads display naturalistic interest. Although the type is not very common in the Hellenistic world the design is typical of its age.

A gold disc earring with cone pendant, from Tarentum, late 4th/early 3rd century BC. Note the elaborate decoration of the disc surmount rendered with filigree rosettes and acanthus leaves. Disc earrings with inverted pyramid or cone pendant were used in certain areas of the Greek world as early as the 6th century BC, but it was in the 4th century that they reached the peak of their popularity. The type remained in favour throughout the Hellenistic period.

A pair of gold and garnet earrings, from Altamura (Bari), late 2nd century BC. Eros, god of love and death with his double funerary and erotic symbolism, is a popular motif in Hellenistic goldsmithwork. He is represented here standing with a vine garland across his shoulders and with a patera in his hands. The surmount is set with a garnet.

A gold earring from Crispiano (Tarentum), circa 375–350 BC, of disc-and-pendant type. The disc supports three pendants, the central one in the shape of a female head, a motif not as common as inverted pyramids and cones. The head presents an interesting peculiarity: a small hole at the base for the insertion of a piece of sponge soaked in perfumed oils. There are almost invisible traces of polychrome enamels, a technique that was to be much used in the Hellenistic period.

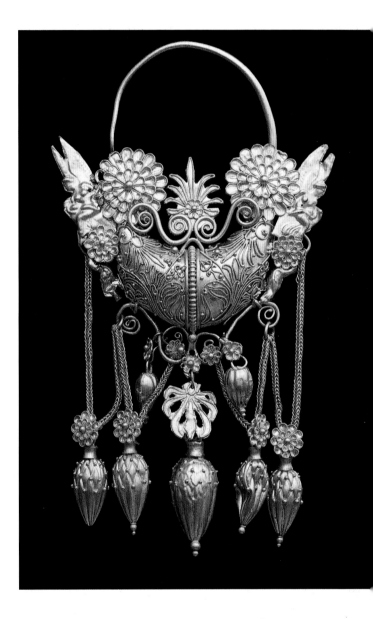

Above: A gold earring of boat-shaped design, from Tarentum, second half of the 4th century BC. The boat motif is enriched with rosettes, nikai and palmette surmounts and is suspended with an elaborate arrangement of chain and pendants. A dramatic chiaroscuro effect is obtained here by the exploitation of gold leaf applications, corded wire, chain and beaded work, replaced in later examples by the use of polychrome enamels.

GREEKS AND ETRUSCANS

Heads on Greek and Roman coins bear witness to the popularity of certain types of earrings, for instance those with vase-shaped pendants. Such earrings appear on Greek vase paintings as early as the 6th century BC.

Above right: A silver *dekadrachm* of Syracuse by Euainetos, circa 400 BC, depicting the head of the water nymph Arethusa surrounded by four dolphins. She wears an earring with vase pendant. And an electrum *tridrachm* of Carthage, 3rd century BC, depicting the head of Tanit wearing an earring with vase pendant, copied from the Euainetos prototype.

Right: Front and side views of an Etruscan gold earring of *a baule* type from Cerveteri, second half of the 6th century BC. The *a baule* type, so called because of its similarity to a travelling case, is typical of Etruria. It consists of a strip of gold leaf bent round to form a cylinder and is often decorated with very fine corded wire and granulation forming geometrical or stylized floral motifs. In this case the decoration is repeated on the side plaque and the elegant palmette surmount. The type was popular throughout Etruria from about 550 BC to about 470 BC and was revived in the 19th century.

Far right: A gold earring, from Volterra, circa 330 BC. Another typically Etruscan form of earring consisting of a horseshoe-shaped surmount supporting a cluster of beads, decorated with corded wire and minute beaded work.

THE RANGE OF ETRUSCAN JEWELLERY

Right: A terracotta statue from Lavinium, first half of the 4th century BC, testifies to the popularity of the Etruscan earring in the form of a horseshoe plaque supporting a cluster of beads, like that shown below centre.

Far right: A gold earring, of uncertain provenance, late 6th century BC, designed as a disc decorated with concentric bands of corded wire and granulation and with rosette motifs at the centre. The origin of this type of earring, or better earstud, is probably to be found in Lydia, from where it spread to Greece proper and Etruria. In Etruria it was particularly fashionable in the second half of the 6th century BC as is confirmed by many tomb paintings at Tarquinia where dancers and ladies banqueting are depicted with disc ear ornaments.

Below: A pair of gold earrings from Spina decorated with heads of the river god Achelous, end of the 5th century BC. Tubular earrings terminating with the heads of men, animals or gods were the most popular form of jewellery in Etruria at the end of the 5th century BC, and were exported to the Adriatic area and to central Europe. With slight variations the type remained popular throughout the 4th and 3rd centuries BC.

Below centre: A gold earring designed as a cluster of beads on a horseshoe surmount, from Vulci, circa 350 BC, stamped out from a single sheet of gold. This is an entirely Etruscan creation popular throughout the region during the 4th and 3rd centuries BC. The globules are hollow inside and act as perfumed oil containers.

Below right: Gold and glass paste earrings from Tarentum, second half of the 2nd century BC. Earrings with a pendant in the shape of a glass paste or enamel bird were particularly popular in Southern Russia and in Italy in the 2nd and 1st centuries BC. Etruscan examples very close to this, dating from 3rd century BC, have been found in Vulci and Chiusi.

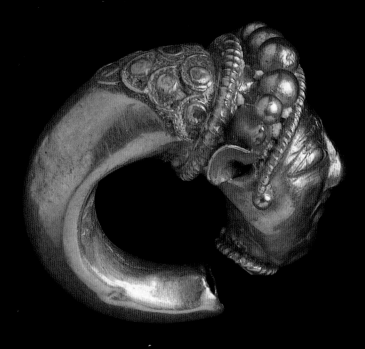 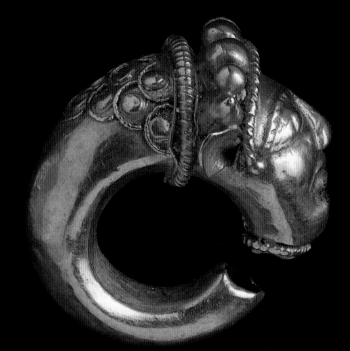

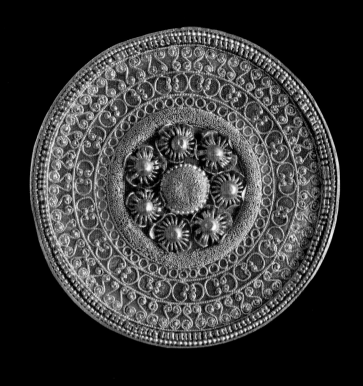

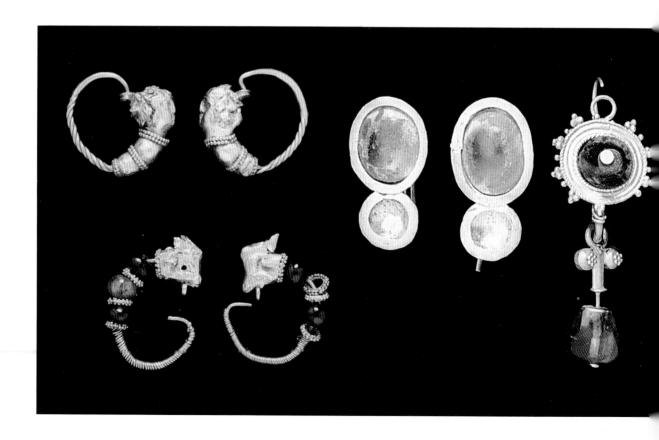

A THOUSAND YEARS OF EARRINGS

Top row, left to right:
A pair of gold earrings of hemispherical design. The S-shaped hooks concealed by smaller bosses. Roman, 2nd century AD, from Cyprus.

A pair of gold earrings, each set with an onyx cameo of a Cupid's head within a reeded gold border. Roman, 2nd century AD. Unknown provenance. The Roman idea of setting hardstone cameos in simple gold earring mounts became a feature of Neoclassicism.

A pair of gold earrings designed as pear-shaped drops set with an amethyst bead within a border of pearls and beaded wire. Early Byzantine, 6th–7th century AD. From Kyrenia, Cyprus.

A pair of gold earrings, each designed as a plain hoop supporting four chains with pearl drops. Early Byzantine, 6th–7th century AD. From Cyprus.

Centre row, left to right:
A pair of crescent-shaped gold earrings, decorated with scrolls of gold wire. Early Byzantine, 7th century AD, from Polis, Cyprus.

A pair of gold earrings of crescent shape, filled with an openwork design of a vase of flowers between two confronted peacocks. The edges are decorated with gold globules. Early Byzantine, 7th century AD, provenance unknown.

A pair of gold earrings of crescent design, decorated with wire motifs of crosses within medallions and scrolls. Early Byzantine period, 7th century AD, from Polis, Cyprus.

Bottom row:
A pair of gold Greek earrings, 4th century BC, with twisted wire hoops and terminals in the form of Maenads' heads.

Two Graeco-Roman gold earrings, probably from Egypt, 1st century BC/1st century AD, with twisted hoops and terminals in the form of the heads of wild goats, decorated with garnet and green glass beads.

A pair of Roman gold earrings, 1st–2nd century a variation of the popular boss earring, with blue enamel inlays at the centre.

A pair of Roman gold and amethyst earrings, 2nd–3rd century AD, the gold and amethyst circular surmount supporting a gold bead and amethyst drop.

A pair of Merovingian earrings, 6th century AD, designed as a large gold hoop decorated with a polyhedral bead inset with garnets. This type is widely spread through Merovingian, Ostrogothic and Southern Russian areas between the 5th and 9th centuries AD, and seems to be the only original form of earring produced in Europe after the fall of the western Roman empire.

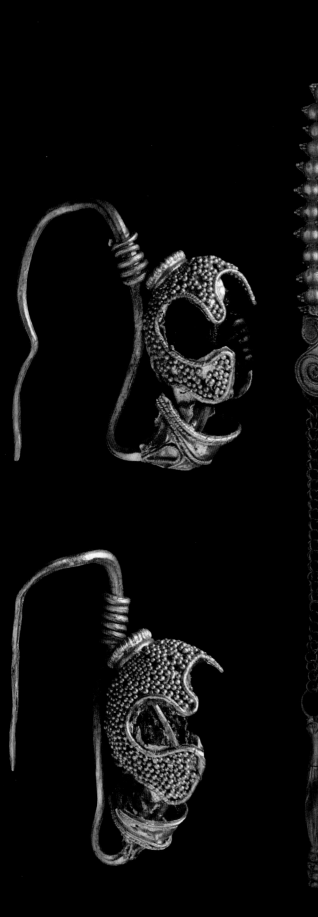

THE GREEK LEGACY TO THE ETRUSCANS

Far left: A pair of gold and amber earrings, from Riparbella, 3rd century BC, designed as negro heads carved in amber, the helmet or headgear decorated with granulation. Hoop earrings decorated at the front with negro heads were very popular in Greek and Etruscan areas in the 3rd century BC. The hook fitting of this Etruscan example is rather uncommon for the type.

Left: A gold earring from Todi, last quarter of the 4th century BC. Designed as an oval boss decorated with filigree and beaded work supporting a female head pendant between chains ending in spindle-shaped drops. An interesting detail is that the female head itself is provided with earrings. The type as a whole derives from Greek prototypes, and shows clear similarities with examples from Tarentum. But this is more than a copy; it is a provincial and overdecorated interpretation, probably created in central Etruria, of more sober and refined Greek or South Italian prototypes. It is very long – over 10.5 cms – but such lengths were not uncommon. Such earrings are made out of thin gold leaf and therefore, although large, are light and reasonably comfortable to wear.

Right above: A pair of gold earrings of disc-and-pendant type from Vulci, 3rd/early 2nd century BC. Disc surmounts decorated with fine granulation support miniature amphorae between pairs of chains terminating with tassels and clusters of beads. Earrings of this type were very fashionable in Etruria at the time and widely diffused throughout the Hellenized world.

Right below: A gold and glass paste earring of disc-and-bird pendant from Tarentum, 2nd century BC. The disc surmount is decorated with white and blue glass paste, the hen pendant rendered in white glass paste. Swans, doves, peacocks and cockerels were favourite shapes for pendent earrings throughout the Hellenistic world, from Southern Russia to Greece, from Etruria to Tarentum.

Portrait of a Young Lady, Dutch, circa 1615, by C. de Vos. The fashion for wing-shaped collars at the beginning of the 17th century permitted pendent earrings to be worn such as those displayed here, which are decorated with pearls and black ribbon bows.

Portrait of a Lady, Dutch, 1650, by Bartholomeus van der Helst, illustrating how at the time long and elaborate diamond-set earrings were being worn.

THE 17TH CENTURY: EARRINGS REVIVED

Although the Renaissance is a particularly rich century for jewellery, earrings were not worn. Elaborate head ornaments or coiffures concealed the ears, especially in Northern Europe, and the fashion for very high ruff collars prevented the use of long and elaborate pendent earrings. It was only in the 17th century that change in both hair and dress fashions determined the reintroduction of large pendent earrings. This is exemplified by the portraits illustrated here.

From left to right
Battista Sforza, Duchess of Urbino, circa 1465, by Piero della Francesca. The Duchess is wearing typically elaborate Italian Renaissance head ornaments: a jewel on the crown of the head and three gem-set brooches fastened to the hair coiled over the ear. (Uffizi, Florence)

Elisabeth Stafford, Lady Drury, English, late 16th century, by Sir William Segar. She is wearing the fashionable high lace ruff collar and hair dressed over paddings to form two puffs concealing the ears.

Barbara Kilingerin, German, 1530, by Hans Maler zu Schwaz. She has her long braids coiled over her ears: a fashionable hairstyle since the late 14th century.

Portrait of a Lady, circa 1660, attributed to the Scottish artist David Scougall. The sitter is shown wearing large and important pendent earrings, each set with a pear-shaped drop on an elaborate diamond and gem-set surmount.

Ann Carr, Countess of Bedford, English, circa 1630, by Sir Anthony van Dyck. The countess wears long earrings, each set with two pear-shaped pearls. This fashionable type of earring was known as the *union d'excellence* and is always characterized by exceptional size and match of the pearls.

THE RETURN OF ELABORATE EARRINGS

Portrait of Anne of Denmark, consort of James I of England, by De Critz (born Antwerp circa 1552–3 – died London 1642). The fashion for open wing-shaped collars and hair swept up on the head prompted the use of long pendent earrings such as those worn by the Queen, each set with a large pear-shaped pearl, connected by a faceted diamond to a red ribbon bow on the surmount. Although long pendent earrings were not worn in Northern Europe until the beginning of the 17th century, in Italy similar earrings, characterized by satin ribbon bows and pearl drops, are already depicted in mid-16th century portraits.

The three designs in pencil, pen and ink, wash body-colour and gold on vellum circa 1610, are by Arnold Lullus, a Netherlands-born jeweller (active circa 1585–circa 1621) greatly favoured by James I of England, the husband of Anne of Denmark. The first consists of a pair of pendent earrings designed as a green enamelled snake from which hangs a ruby within a white enamel crescent supporting three green drops. The second is similar, presenting a green enamel snake suspending a single diamond, a crescent in white enamel set with faceted diamonds and a single green drop. The third is set with eleven table-cut diamonds in a polychrome enamel openwork border supporting two pearl drops and a green gemstone. All three are characteristic of the early 17th century for their size, elaboration of design, interest in enamel-work and faceted gemstones, a consequence of the improved gem-cutting techniques of the time.

GEMS OF THE BAROQUE

Front and back views of a pair of gold, enamel, emerald, ruby and pearl pendent earrings, first half of the 17th century. The front is set with faceted gemstones; the back is painted with red and black enamel depicting three tulips on a light blue ground.

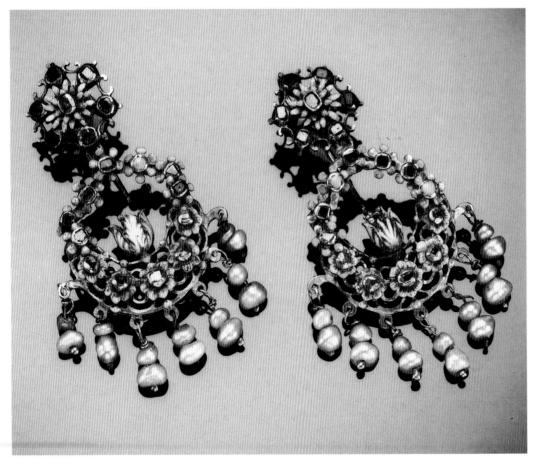

A pair of gold, polychrome enamel, ruby, turquoise and diamond pendent earrings, circa 1640. Each is designed as an openwork garland of floral motifs carrying a fringe of pearls, the centre decorated with a red and white tulip, and suspended on a flowerhead cluster surmount.

What is noticeable in both these examples, besides the intricacy of design, is the interest in floral patterns, especially the tulip, which had become one of the favourite flower motifs of the time following the 'tulipomania' of the years around 1634.

2

The age of elegance:
earrings in the 18th century

The girandole

By the beginning of the 18th century earrings had become an essential form of adornment.

The girandole, first seen around the middle of the 17th century, remained the most popular type of earring. As we have seen, it consisted of a surmount, usually a bow motif, with three pear-shaped drops, the larger one at the centre, suspended from a hook. The hook allowed the drops to be detached, so that the surmount could be worn on its own when occasion required it.

There are several explanations for the popularity of the girandole. The first has to do with fashion in clothes and hair. During the 18th century hair was worn gathered up on the head away from the face, leaving the ears uncovered; and the low cut of dresses for formal occasions left the area around the neck and ears perfectly suited for adornment with earrings. Secondly, earrings and particularly girandoles exploited the qualities of faceted stones, especially diamonds, which had become plentiful after their discovery in Brazil in 1723; before that the supply had been limited to the mines of Golconda in India. Also significant was the improvement in techniques for cutting diamonds: around 1700 it is thought that the Venetian Vincenzo Peruzzi devised the brilliant-cut, a cut that enhanced the optical properties of diamonds, enabling the stone to reflect light and sparkle at its best. The new brilliant-cut diamonds were particularly successful when mounted on girandole earrings with the stones hanging freely on both sides of the face and catching the light. Thirdly, improved domestic candles meant that more social occasions could be held at night, and in these circumstances sparkling diamond-set jewels and especially girandoles were particularly effective. Until the mid-18th century, jewellery was set solely with diamonds. For formal evening occasions, diamond girandole earrings were all the rage, while during the day girandoles set with more sober semiprecious stones such as garnets, cornelians, pearls, aventurine glass and pastes were preferred. For the first time in the history of jewellery a differentiation was made between day-time and night-time jewels, a distinction which remains to this day.

. 50, 51
The girandole remained the favoured type of earring throughout the 18th century and in general terms its basic elements – the bow surmount and drops, the emphasis on width rather than length and the practice of wearing matching bodice ornaments called sévignés – are features which had been common since the 17th century. There are, however, certain small differences. The early 18th-century girandole may be distinguished from its 17th-century counterpart mainly by its emphasis on the faceted stones rather than on the setting and enamel-work; in the 17th century the setting was decorated at the front and back with poychrome enamels and engravings, but towards the end of that century enamel-work and engraving were confined to the back and disappeared completely at the beginning of the 18th.

Elements remaining from the 17th century include the rather stiff design with the clearly defined bow and drops as separate units, and the pronounced horizontal development, stressing width rather than length. Such features are clearly visible in the designs engraved by Quien dated 1710 and published posthumously in London in p. 57 1762, especially the stiffness of the design, the drop treated as separate elements, the horizontality and the interest in the faceted stone.

Girandoles were popular throughout Europe at the beginning of the 18th century, p. 50, 51 but there are small differences which betray their country of origin. In France they were set entirely with diamonds and were characterized by a sense of movement and sculptural quality. In Spain they were sturdier and set typically with a combination of emeralds and diamonds, a fact explained by the relatively easy supply of emeralds from mines in Colombia, which belonged to Spain. Portuguese girandoles were characterized by simple and flat lines and were usually set with topazes and chrysoberyls from Brazil, then a Portuguese colony. In the Adriatic regions and especially Southern Italy girandoles were given bold outlines and were frequently set with seed pearls as opposed to gemstones.

Girandoles of the second half of the 18th century show some slight changes. In France, particularly, they were no longer set only with diamonds but with a combination of diamonds and coloured gemstones such as rubies. Secondly, they gradually develop a more vertical outline with a more elongated central drop, noticeable in the Italian designs of circa 1770 and exemplified by the proportions set out in the *Principes de Giraindoles* designed and engraved by Van der Creusen in 1770. And thirdly, the basic bow surmount is frequently replaced by a more complex arrangement, for example the combination of ribbon bow and flower spray motif seen in the ruby and diamond girandoles and in Pouget's designs for girandoles, dated 1762. One of his p. 57 pages, for instance, shows six different designs for girandoles. The four set with pearls display intricate motifs in the centre other than bows: a floral motif, two hearts, paired doves and a trophy of love with two hearts and arrows. The characteristic intricacy of the central element is evident also in the emerald and diamond examples from Spain; the centre in the form of a flowerhead cluster is set with a large emerald

Principes de Girandoles

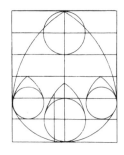

Engraved design of the 'Principes de Girandoles' by L. Van der Cruycen, 1770, showing the proportions of a girandole earring.

Engraved designs for three pearl girandole earrings by L. Van der Cruycen, 1770. The central motifs are flower sprays.

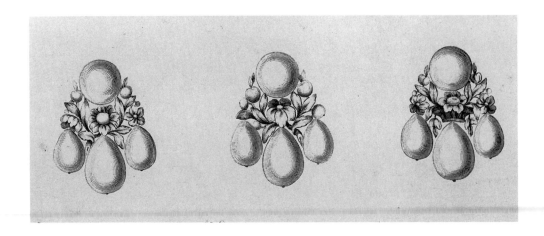

in a border of rose diamonds framed by diamond-set foliate spray motifs. The other typical feature of late 18th-century girandoles is the working together of the surmount and drops into much more of an ensemble, compared to the early girandoles where they are treated as separate units.

Most girandoles were quite large, and weight was an important aspect which should not be overlooked. It depended on two features, the size of the earring and the setting of the stones. Gemstones were commonly mounted in closed settings with collets closed at the back, which were lined with coloured foils to enhance the colour of the stones and improve the evenness of colour; in the case of diamonds, foils gave a subtle hue to the stones. Gold was used to set coloured stones while silver was normally used to set diamonds, as it suited their whiteness. So much metal was used in the setting that the earrings were inevitably very heavy, something which is stressed by the designer and engraver Augustin Duflos in the 'Discours Preliminere' to his p. 56 *Recueil des Dessins*, published in 1744. The need to alleviate the weight of girandole earrings led to the introduction of a special fitting, consisting of penannular wire hinged on one side to be inserted from back to front into the pierced earlobe. An additional loop soldered off-centre at the top held a ribbon secured to the hair, taking some of the weight off the ears. The Spanish emerald and diamond girandoles illustrated here are approximately 39 grams; today an average of about 22 grams per earring is reckoned to be as heavy as a woman can comfortably wear.

Tolerance of heavy earrings depends, of course, on how long they are worn, how much movement is involved and how the weight is distributed. When the weight of a long earring is concentrated in a small area, it will feel much heavier than when the p. 57 same weight is spread over a larger surface, as in the case of a disc. Duflos mentions this problem of weight. 'Ladies', he says, 'are the principal objects of the Jeweller's Art, who mainly devotes his work to them. If this work, by chance, falls under their hands, it might perhaps bring them back to noble and simple taste, better suited in differentiating them and in showing their natural graces than the glittering display that has been favoured for some time. Then they will reduce, by their own accord, the enormous size of Flowers and Girandole Earrings, which tires the ears and they will prefer beautiful diamonds, although smaller in size, to a disorderly cluster of small stones which add up to a lot of weight and are ill suited.'

The pendeloque

Another type of earring which became popular in the second half of the 18th century, p. 52, 53 although it was well established fifty years earlier, was the pendeloque. Its design is characterized by a marquise-shaped surmount supporting a central ribbon bow motif and an elongated drop of a design similar to the surmount, frequently decorated with p. 57 a swing centre. Variations include one model which has a more elaborate central section with a combination of bow and floral spray motifs, and pear-shaped drops. The pendeloque seems to have come into fashion because its elongated outline counterbalanced the extreme height of hairstyles around the 1770s. This style reached its peak among the upper classes in 1778. A pad made of wool, hemp and wire was placed on the head and either natural or horse hair with pomade and powder was stretched over. They must have been extremely uncomfortable and unhygienic, since they were often kept in place for weeks at a time, becoming breeding grounds for lice and fleas; furthermore, they were highly impractical, obstructing one's view and making it difficult to fit into a coach. Caricaturists showed servants employed to hold up the weight of the hair, or attending to their mistress's hair from ladders, and ladies travelling in carriages with the roof opened up for the high coiffures to stick out. But comfort was not the main concern of the fashionable lady; she delighted in the way the sweeping high line of her hair was perfectly counterbalanced by the elongated drops of her pendeloque earrings.

Most of the pendeloques were set with diamonds but few have survived, since the settings were melted down and the stones reset. The great majority of extant examples are set with colourless pastes or crystals such as white topazes and rock crystal imitating diamonds. The interest in imitation diamonds is typical of the 18th century; and paste jewellery of this period can be considered the forerunner of modern luxury costume jewellery. Another favourite type of pendeloque besides those set with dia- p. 52, 53, 58, 59

'A Hint to the Ladies to take Care of their HEADS', a satirical print of 1776.

p. 49

p. 57

monds or pastes is the one with a pear-shaped pearl drop usually set as a swing centre in a diamond-set frame. In design books one frequently finds variations of girandoles and pendeloques illustrated together. In those of Quien (dated 1710) and Saint (dated 1759), there are engravings of three variations of girandoles and six slightly differing pendeloques all on the same page. Similarly, in the designs of Maria, active 1751–70, eight variations of girandoles and three pendeloques are depicted.

Pendeloques were set in much the same way as girandoles with the stones mounted in closed collets, but they were lighter, having a single drop from the bow surmount instead of three. This explains why one frequently finds a different fitting; instead of the hook with additional loop to alleviate the weight, there is a plain long S-shaped wire hook soldered to the surmount of the earrings. This is clearly depicted in some coloured designs of pendeloques (1760–70) by an anonymous Italian jeweller, in the Victoria and Albert Museum in London.

The 'two-stone' earring

Another popular mid to late 18th-century earring is the type known as the 'two-stone' earring. This consists of two large oval faceted gemstones, the larger one on top, with the plane joining the two embellished with various decorative motifs. The simplest version of this decoration comprises just two small lozenge-shaped stones filling in the gaps at the sides where the two larger stones meet; the more elaborate type, as seen in Duflos' engraved designs of 1744, presents lateral floral and foliate spray motifs. This type of earring was suited for the display of large and important stones, especially diamonds, but hardly any examples have survived, because such large and important stones tend inevitably to be reset in more up-to-date settings. The extant examples mostly contain pastes and garnets and have survived because there was no advantage in melting them down and resetting the gemstones. Nevertheless even the low value 'two-stone' earrings are very attractive: a pair set with translucent blue opaline paste may be seen in the Museum of London; it is also interesting to note how sometimes the simple 'two-stone' motif is repeated to form a necklace usually worn en suite with the earrings.

From the 18th century onwards, girandoles and pendoloques continued in favour, though modified as one could expect to meet changing tastes. One finds a variation of the girandole in the 1830s and again in the late 1920s, while the pendeloque enjoyed particular favour in the 1820s and 1880s.

A lasting tradition

In certain peripheral areas, however, fashion evolves more slowly than in courtly and international circles, and the form of the girandole and the pendeloque has remained

p. 63

virtually unchanged from the 18th century to modern times. This can clearly be seen in provincial jewellery of the Iberian peninsula where one finds a recurring girandole design: a central stylized bow motif with three pear-shaped drops, pierced in gold

Engraved designs by J. D. Saint, for three girandoles and two pendeloque earrings, 1759.

Two types of earring dominate the 18th century: the pendeloque and the girandole. Pendeloque earrings had been in favour since the early part of the century, but their greatest popularity came in the 1770s. Their basic design consisted of a circular or oval surmount supporting an elongated drop which counterbalanced the excessively high hairstyles of that time. The pair shown here represent one of the commonest of the many variants. A diamond and pearl cluster supports a diamond ribbon bow motif suspended with a pear-shaped diamond drop with a pearl swing centre.

decorated with small rose diamonds. Dating these earrings can be problematic. Earlier examples have engraved scrolling on the back, while later ones are stamped out from a die and are coarser in appearance. They are frequently accompanied by a bodice ornament of ribbon bow known as a 'laca' which derives from the traditional p. 55 sévigné. These Iberian examples are not particularly heavy, having pierced mounts and being set with fewer stones; this explains the fitting which, unlike the conventional 18th-century girandole, consists of a gold hinged hook which is inserted into the ear from back to front without any additional supporting device.

Other pendeloques follow closely the traditional 18th-century prototypes. Some have a ribbon bow and pear-shaped drop, others a much more elongated pendant, as long as 8 cms. A typical Portuguese earring derived from the pendeloque is the 'Brincos a Rainha', 'Queen's earring'. It has a bow surmount and a swing centre, but the drop is usually wider and stones are replaced by faceted gold bead motifs. All our examples are made from a sheet of high carat gold (usually 20 carat) from which the design has been cut out by means of a saw and file, producing a lace-like effect. Inlays were skilfully chiselled by hand and the collets that were placed round the stones, usually rose diamonds, were made separately and embellished by the burin. Later examples in the 19th century were frequently cast in the chosen shape and then finished with the chisel and burin.

In another area of the Iberian peninsula centred around Catalonia, during the late 18th century, the girandole was the inspiration for the design of the extremely popular 'Catalan earring', which remained in vogue virtually unmodified up to the end p. 54, 6 of the 19th century. Unlike the Portuguese examples, Catalan earrings are extremely long and resemble late 18th-century Spanish girandoles. They are mounted with an abundance of gemstones in closed settings and chased mounts. The stones are never diamonds but semiprecious stones such as hessonite garnets and amethysts. The central ribbon bow motif is greatly stylized, the emphasis being on length rather than width, and all the elements are integrated into the overall design. Some examples have a very large central drop flanked by two smaller ones, thus retaining the structure of the girandole, while others have only a single large drop and are closer in conception to the pendeloque. The long popularity of this type of earring in Catalonia is demonstrated by numerous surviving examples and by its frequent appearance even in 19th-century portraits, e.g., the *Flower Woman from Valencia* by Joaquim Argasot p. 60 y Juan. The sitter is wearing typical Catalan earrings mounted in gold with dark green gemstones, the usual stylized ribbon bow surmount suspending three drops; they are so long that they nearly rest on the shawl draped over the woman's shoulders. Indeed, these Catalan earrings could measure up to 14 cms and were often so heavy that they had to be supported by an additional hook placed over the ear. Sidney Churchill, in an article on 'Peasant Jewellery' published in *The Studio*, mentions the practice of alleviating the weight of a heavy earring by means of a ribbon tied round the ear, which he saw in Nicosia as late as 1912.

THE TRIUMPH OF THE GIRANDOLE

The other most characteristic form of earring of the 18th century was the girandole, which was fashionable throughout the whole of Europe. In the early 18th century it tended to have a horizontal shape, the three drops more or less of the same size and at the same level, and the central motif clearly defined and simple in design. Later it became more vertical in emphasis with a longer and larger central drop and a more elaborate central motif.

Above and opposite right: Late 18th-century girandole earrings from Spain, set with emeralds and diamonds, a characteristic feature of Spanish jewellery. The elaborate central motif combines ribbon bow and spray of flowers

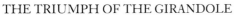

Centre top: French, circa 1760s, set with foiled rubies and diamonds, the drops and the central motif articulated. The combination of rubies and diamonds and the elaborate bow motif place it in the second half of the century.

Middle: English, second half of the 18th century, set with foiled garnets. Note the rather stiff design and the clearly defined ribbon motif. The colour of the garnets is enhanced by bright pink foiling.

Bottom: Portuguese, circa 1750, set with foiled topazes. The choice of the gemstones – topazes from Brazil, then a colony of Portugal – and the linear and flat design are typical of Portuguese jewellery.

THE ELEGANT PENDELOQUE

A collection of late 18th-century silver
and diamond pendeloque earrings. These
examples show some of the many
variations of the pendeloque design, from
the cluster, ribbon bow and pear-shaped
drop (*right and opposite above*) to the
articulated and elaborate swing centre
(*centre and opposite below*). Note the use of
silver as setting metal to complement the
whiteness of diamonds. As is normal at
this time, all gemstones are mounted in
closed settings.

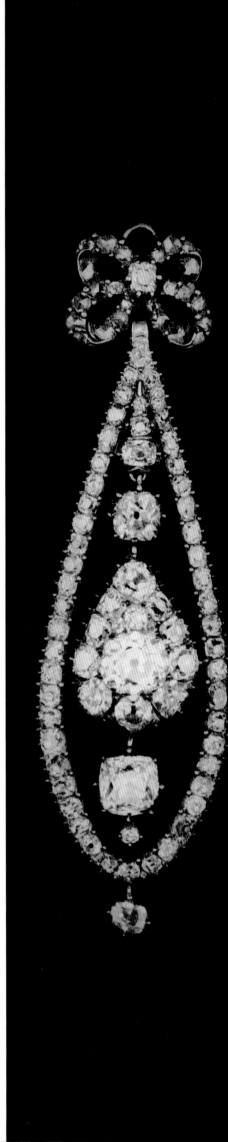

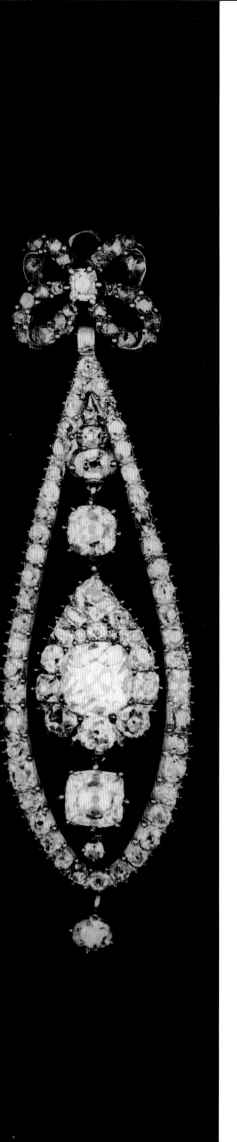

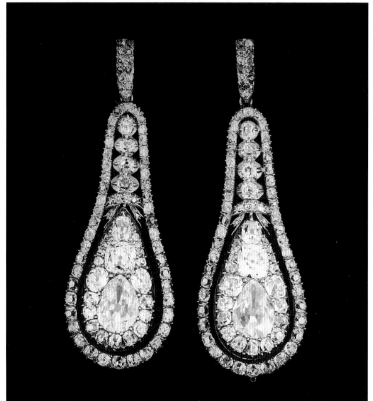

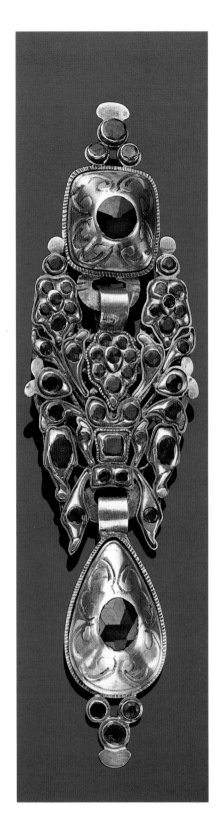

IBERIAN STYLE

Right: A gold and hessonite garnet earring, Catalan, probably early 19th century. The striking design is a development of the traditional pendeloque design with a cluster surmount, an elaborate floral spray centre and an elongated pear-shaped drop. Many examples are extremely long and heavy, requiring special mounts to support their weight.

Opposite right: A collection of 18th- and 19th-century gold earrings, Portuguese and Spanish. These earrings exemplify the persistence, in the Ibérian peninsula, of the pendeloque motif based on surmount, ribbon bow and elongated drop. The great variety of design includes the traditional pendeloque conceived as a cluster surmount set with emeralds or rose diamonds supporting a bow and a pear-shaped drop; the 'Brincos a Rainha' with its wide, almost circular, drop with swing centre, entirely pierced in high carat gold; the elongated spindle-shaped earrings chased in gold with scroll motifs known as 'Fuso', and the bow pendants (centre of page).

Detail of a portrait of Mary, Countess of Macclesfield, by Francis Coates, exhibited at the Society of Artists in 1763 and much admired by Horace Walpole. The Countess is wearing fashionable diamond girandole earrings.

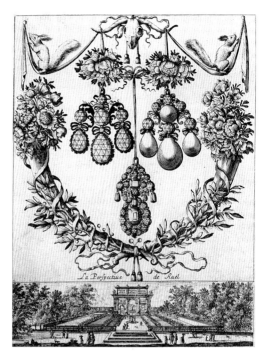

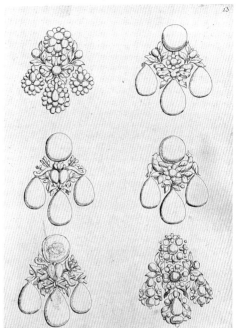

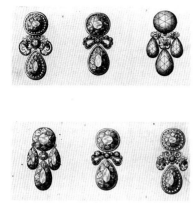

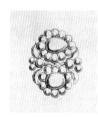

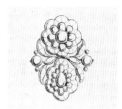

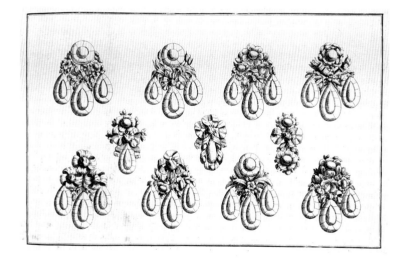

REFINEMENTS OF THE 18TH CENTURY

Opposite far left: A Portuguese silver and white topaz earring of girandole design, first half of the 18th century, and (*below*) front and back view of a diamond girandole earring mounted in silver. The back view shows three typical features of the girandole: the closed setting of the stones; the articulated and detachable drops that allow the earring to be worn in a reduced form; and the additional hoop, through which a ribbon was threaded and secured to the hair.

This page:
Illustrations from 18th-century literature on earrings.
Top: An extract from the 'Discours Preliminaire' of the *Recueil des Dessins* by A. Duflos, 1744, where the author expresses his concern about the excessive weight and elaborate design of girandole earrings. *Above, left to right:* French engraved designs of two girandole earrings and one pendeloque earring by F. LeFebvre (active circa 1635–57); a page of French engraved designs for six girandoles by Pouget, 1762; six engraved designs for pendeloques and girandoles by J. Quien, 1710, published posthumously in London in 1762; and two designs for a two-stone or double-cluster earring, by Duflos, 1744, a fashionable form that cannot be classified as either girandole or pendeloque.

Centre left: A page of French designs by Maria, 1751–70, engraved by Babel, illustrating fashionable pendeloques and girandoles.

Below left: Four engraved designs for pendeloque and girandole earrings, by an anonymous Italian, circa 1770.

THE PENDELOQUE: THEME AND VARIATIONS

Centre right: An unusual and colourful pair of earrings, late 18th century, set with cornelian plaques within diamond borders.

Right: A pair of diamond pendent earrings, Russian, mid-18th century. The interest in large cushion-shaped brilliant-cut diamonds mounted in closed silver settings is a typical 18th-century feature.

Opposite: Four pairs of pendeloque earrings mounted in silver or gold and silver with colourless gemstones such as white topazes and rock crystal.

Opposite far right: A pair of diamond pendeloque earrings, English, late 18th century. Note the large rose diamonds in silver closed settings and the rather severe design typical of many English creations of the time. And (*bottom far right*) a pair of topaz pendeloque earrings and a matching *devant de corsage*, Portuguese, mid-18th century, interesting for its combination of light yellow and foiled orange stones.

Below: A collection of English diamond jewellery, late 18th century, comprising typical pendeloque earrings and a flowerhead dress ornament.

OUT OF THE MAINSTREAM

Below: A mid 19th-century portrait by Joaquin Argasot y Juan of a Spanish lady wearing a pair of large gold and gem-set earrings of girandole inspiration, proving how long earrings of this type continued to be popular in the Iberian Peninsula. Their size explains why additional fittings were required.

Right: Silver and rose diamond pendeloque earrings, probably Flemish; and gold Iberian earrings set with topazes, of modified girandole design, similar to those in the portrait above.

Opposite, top left to bottom right: Gold and gem-set Spanish earrings, a variation of the Catalan type but with a much more slender outline; Catalan earrings; gold Iberian earrings set with emeralds; and garnet Catalan earrings. All on this page late 18th/early 19th century.

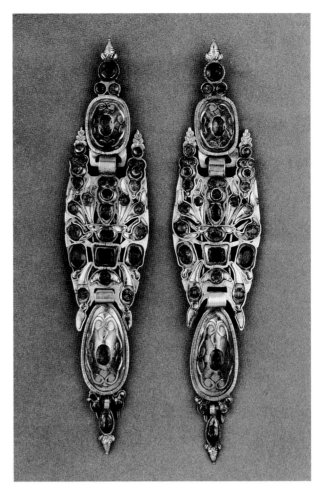

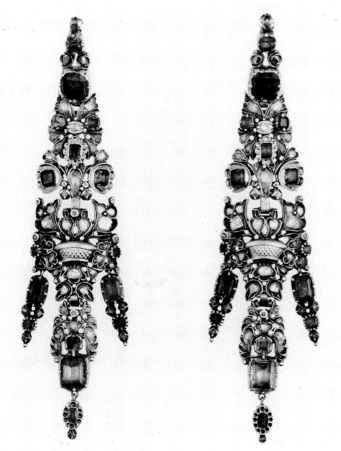

Below: A pair of seed pearl and ruby girandole earrings, Southern Italian, mid-18th century. The use of minute seed pearls threaded on a filigree structure is a typical feature of many Southern Italian and Adriatic jewels of low intrinsic value. Even so the design presents the most typical features of the girandole: cluster surmount, bow and detachable drops.

Opposite: A pair of gilt-metal and glass girandole earrings, probably Italian mid-18th century, using copper coloured aventurine glass with gold spangles cut and faceted as if it were a precious stone. Glass paste of various colours was frequently cut and set in 18th-century day jewellery, and even aristocratic ladies who owned precious jewels did not disdain to wear it. The smaller pictures show two pairs of Iberian earrings set respectively with rose diamonds and emeralds, late 18th century. One is modelled on the traditional girandole, the other on the pendeloque form, which in this region retained their popularity well into the 19th century.

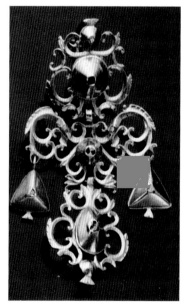

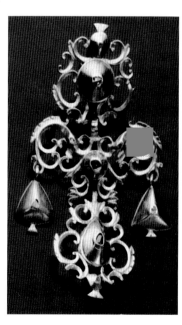

A pair of spectacular Southern Italian gold and seed pearl pendent earrings, late 18th
century. Although this particular type seems to be confined to Southern Italy and the
Adriatic regions, its structure conforms to the contemporary pendeloque design. The use
of seed pearls had been a typical feature of jewels of this area since the 17th century,
providing an extremely successful and decorative alternative to jewels set with precious
gemstones.

3

The 19th century:
riches and revivals

The French Revolution in 1789 brought a temporary halt to the output of precious jewels in the country which had until then been the leading producer. Ostentatious adornment was felt to conflict with the revolutionary principles of egalitarism. Moreover, the abolition of the traditional guild system, which in the past had ensured a high standard by regulating the terms of apprenticeship, led to a rapid decline in quality. And finally there was a lack of patronage and a scarcity of precious metals and gemstones. Many French aristocrats, the traditional patrons of French jewellers, fled the country, taking their valuables to sell abroad as a means of livelihood. French jewellers were therefore deprived both of old jewels with gems and precious metals for re-setting and of new imported bullion and gemstones. It was during this time of upheaval that the prized French crown jewels were stolen.

From the French Revolution to Waterloo
Not surprisingly, earrings created at this time reflect the impoverishment of design and production; only inexpensive examples of low artistic value based on Revolutionary motifs are to be found. One design used glass and debris from the demolished Bastille. Another commonly known as *boucle d'oreille à la guillotine*, and favoured in Nantes rather than Paris, consisted of a small guillotine surmounted by a red cap, with a pendant below in the form of a decapitated crowned head.

Fine jewellery staged a gradual comeback during the years of the Directory (1795–99); France began to recover its leadership in the field; new motifs and designs were developed, remaining in favour until the early 19th century.

The new earrings, in line with the general interest in classicism, were designed to complement the 'à la Grècque' hairstyles and the fashion for flimsy white dresses inspired by Classical goddesses. (Indeed, the passion for pale, flimsy chemise-dresses with drapery clinging to the body was so great that some ladies even wore their clothes wet to enhance the effect. As a consequence there was an increase in deaths from pneumonia.) Fashionable earrings of the period were usually large and geometrical, with the emphasis on flat linearity rather than volume. Although quite large, they were usually very light; gold was still scarce and earrings would be cut out of thin sheets, frequently of low carat gold; enamel often took the place of gemstones. Once again, this tendency can be explained partly by the general scarcity of stones on the market, partly by a desire to create earrings which would complement the face without overpowering it with an excess of jewels.

Between 1790 and 1810 two main types can be distinguished. The first is known as the *poissarde*, so called because it was originally worn by fishwives (*poissardes*) in the market of Les Halles in Paris. It is characterized by a hinged fitting at the back, either semicircular or S-shaped, running from bottom to top, where it fastens to the front section of the earring. The front is usually in the form of a flat panel or half-

. 90, 91

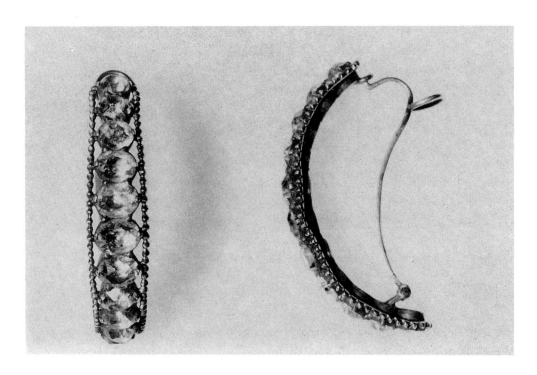

A pair of *poissarde* earrings set with citrines, early 19th century, front and side view. Note the S-shaped hinged fitting running from top to bottom.

hoop decorated with enamel, often pierced and set with a few imitation or semi-precious stones. The second type is a long pendent earring with a combination of flat and extremely thin gold elements linked to each other by means of fine chains. As with the *poissardes* they are hardly ever set with precious stones but are decorated with polychrome enamel, pierced gold and filigree. One example incorporates marquise-shaped surmounts decorated respectively with *grisaille* miniature portraits of man and wife in profile on a light blue enamel ground. A double chain connects the surmount with a central element decorated with sentimental imagery: a dove above a pair of red enamel flaming hearts, followed by the inscription *Fidel* in a garland of blue forget-me-nots and red leaves. Though typical of early 19th-century earrings, and probably French, to judge from the inscription, the sentimental imagery is an unusual feature. Earrings, unlike other forms of jewellery, are normally purely decorative and hardly ever display the explicitly sentimental motifs which are often found on rings – the traditional symbol of love and eternal union, and a normal betrothal gift since Antiquity.

Earrings of these two types were worn throughout Europe, not only in France. Maria de la Concepcion Rodriguez de Caspe, a lady from Granada, for example, was painted by José Gil in 1816 wearing earrings that have two circular elements each set with a red unfaceted stone, probably coral, connected by fine chains. Once again the typical linearity, lack of volume and absence of precious gemstones are noticeable. Similar examples were also extensively produced in Sicily and in Northern Italy; some measure over 8 cms in length and still remain light, being made of thin 18 carat

p. 89 gold sheets and weighing on average 7 grams. Northern Italian earrings display some distinctive features, in particular a plaque stamped out of a thin circular, oval or rectangular sheet of gold. This is decorated at the centre in relief to simulate a cameo, with the profile of a warrior from Classical mythology. Classical martial imagery, such as Mars and Bellona, both war-deities, were popular subjects during Napoleon's campaigns in Northern Italy of 1796–97. The borders, however, present a characteristic form of decoration with small hollow hemispherical motifs imitating beaded wirework, filigree, palmette and flowerhead motifs.

The coronation of Napoleon in 1804 and the creation of a grand Imperial court prompted demand for extremely important jewels. The overall design of earrings remained unchanged, but gold and enamel were replaced by precious stones, diamonds being again in favour. p. 90 This can clearly be seen in a pair of diamond pendent earrings, where the general design continues to be long and linear, but fine connecting chains, typical of the earlier gold earrings, have been replaced by a grand chain of brilliant-cut diamonds.

Until the closing years of the 18th century gemstones had always been mounted in closed settings which did not allow light to pass from behind through the stone. This technique enabled the jewellers to match, modify and intensify the tint of coloured gemstones by placing coloured foils behind the stone, but this greatly reduced the sparkle and brilliance of diamonds. Towards 1800 jewellers, realizing the importance of light for the glitter of diamonds, started to claw- or collet-set them in open mounts, although smaller and rose-cut diamonds and coloured stones continued to be mounted in closed settings. Many pendent earrings of this time are transitional in type, with a large diamond, usually the centre stone, mounted in an open setting and smaller stones, generally in the border, in closed setting.

By the early 19th century, French supremacy in jewellery design had been re-established. This was largely due to Napoleon's enthusiasm for the development of French arts and technology. He regarded the luxury of his court as an aspect of national prestige, not mere frivolity. This led to an immense number of commissions for jewellery, which was then distributed throughout Europe as diplomatic gifts.

It is at this time that complete sets of matching jewels known as parures begin to be worn. They consisted of a necklace, bracelets, a pair of pendent earrings and frequently also a tiara. Amidst such an abundance of gemstones, earrings continued to be simple, the favourites being long pearl or diamond pendeloques on small surmounts; they can be seen being worn by the Empress Joséphine and other members of the imperial family in portraits by David, Gérard and Regnault. Another favoured type consists of a cluster with a large gemstone or cameo at the centre within a border of pearls or diamonds, often holding a similarly set pear-shaped drop. This is well represented by a pair of diamond and emerald briolette earrings, part of·the parure probably by Nitot given by Napoleon to Stephanie Beauharnais, a niece of the Empress Joséphine, on the occasion of her marriage in 1806. (This is an example of the political role of jewellery; she was marrying the Grand Duke of Baden's heir, an alliance intended to consolidate the Confederacy of the Rhine.) This parure is now in the Victoria and Albert Museum in London, and the bride is portrayed wearing it in a painting by Gérard. The popularity of earrings set with cameos, carved both in shell and hardstone and occasionally in precious stones such as emeralds and sapphires, was a consequence of Napoleon's personal interest in precious stones. Following the Italian campaigns of 1796, when many cameos were brought back to France from Italy, Napoleon opened in Paris a school of gem engraving which boosted the production of cameos of Classical inspiration which were then frequently set in earrings.

1815–1830

The Congress of Vienna brought about the restoration of the legitimate monarchs in Europe in 1815, and with it the desire to emulate the style of the Ancien Regime in all the applied arts. In jewellery earrings reverted to the form of 18th-century girandoles and pendeloques, but they were adapted to the more impoverished economic situation. The scarcity of precious metals and gemstones prompted the development of filigree and cannetille which allowed jewellers to make do with very little gold. Both cannetille, named after a type of embroidery made with very fine gold and silver thread, and filigree techniques consist of working fine gold wires into lace-work patterns. Long but light pendeloque and girandole earrings manufactured on the Continent in this way were mainly set with semiprecious stones such as foiled topazes, amethysts and citrines. In England, which had been spared the consequences of the war, more expensive gemstones such as emeralds, diamonds and rubies (but never sapphires at this period) mounted in cannetille settings were often used. These gemstones are almost invariably set in closed collets lined with metallic foils tinted to intensify the colour and improve the match of the stones. The earrings are usually found as part of parures, accompanied by a pair of bracelets and a necklace with a detachable pendant at the centre designed to match the earrings either as a girandole, or, when the earrings are designed as pendeloques, in the form of a lozenge or Latin cross. These parures were extremely popular in the 1820s and early 1830s: their gold filigree work of burr, tendrils, scrolls and lace-like patterns was often embellished with leaves and florets stamped out of thin gold sheet sometimes in contrasting colours. The two exceptional English examples illustrated, set with rubies and emeralds both comprising a necklace with girandole pendant and a pair of matching earrings, are particularly notable for the quality of the gemstones and for the pristine condition of the cannetille work, something which has rarely survived intact because of its lightness and fragility. The overall design of the girandoles, elongated in shape and with the central drop longer thn the two at the sides, is close to late 18th-century examples, but the cartouche-shaped surmount of the example set with emeralds, the parsimonious use of gemstones and the fine intricacy of light gold wire and granulation make them typical of their date.

P. 73

P. 94

Portrait of a lady wearing a pair of long pendent earrings set with faceted semiprecious gemstone drops, to counterbalance the side expansion of the elaborate hairstyles fashionable in the 1830s. By Adèle Kindt (Belgian 1804–1884).

The 1830s

Around the 1830s long earrings reaching almost the shoulders became extremely popular. The fashion was prompted by changes in dress and hairstyle. Couturiers of the time had launched the fashion for dresses with wide bell-shaped skirts, narrow waists and leg-of-mutton sleeves which expanded sideways out of all proportion, giving the upper part of the female silhouette a marked triangular shape. The head became the focal point of interest for jewellers and milliners: hairstyles became extremely complex, with tight curls and knots of false and natural hair gathered at the top and side of the head and embellished with all sorts of feathers, plumes and jewelled aigrettes. This exaggerated horizontal expansion of female silhouette and overabundance of hairstyle decoration needed to be counterbalanced by long drop earrings which also well suited the very generous decolletages of evening dresses.

The most fashionable earrings of the time were designed as elongated drops measuring up to 10–12 cms in length stamped out of thin gold sheet and decorated *en*

p. 74

A gold cannetille and aquamarine parure comprising a necklace, a lozenge-shaped pendant and a pair of pendeloque earrings, circa 1830. Gold cannetille, named after a type of embroidery made of gold and silver thread, consists of working very fine gold wires into lace-like patterns embellished with burr, floret and bead motifs. This technique became extremely popular between 1820 and 1830 when the scarcity of gold on the market prompted jewellers to economize. Fashion required earrings to be long, and cannetille earrings had the advantage of being very light. Cannetille parures always comprise long earrings but they vary in shape to match the pendant of the necklace: lozenge-shaped pendants are in most cases accompanied by pendeloque earrings, girandole pendants by similarly designed earrings.

repoussé (embossed); their rich scroll, shell and foliate motifs were often applied with minute naturalistic decorative elements in gold of various colours and set with gems. A good example of this type is the pair of torpedo-shaped earrings reproduced on p. 93, decorated with embossed quatrefoil motifs suspended from a shell-shaped surmount.

Some of the earliest examples of *repoussé* earrings are also decorated with applied cannetille motifs in the form of burr and scrolling tendrils and can be regarded as transitional between cannetille and *repoussé* earrings.

By the early 1840s gold *repoussé* earrings had completely supplanted the costly and p. 74, 7 time-consuming cannetille type. Their lightness was dictated partly by economic considerations and partly by the necessity of keeping such large earrings light and comfortable for the wearer. *Repoussé* earrings were cheap to produce. They were made on mechanical presses and needed only very thin sheets of precious metal, though the *repoussé* work itself was often set with small semiprecious gemstones, turquoises being among the favourites.

If a large stone was used, it was likely to be aquamarine, chrysoberyl, amethyst, topaz or citrine, set within a scrolled border of rich gold *repoussé* work. The aquamarine drops reproduced on p. 95 exemplify the trend particularly well, in that they are extremely long (12 cms approximately) and light (weighing approximately 15 grams each) and are set with Brazilian aquamarines of fancy cut, well adapting to the *repoussé* scroll-motif mount.

In Switzerland and Northern Italy, where enamel techniques were mastered at the time, polychrome enamel plaques could replace gemstones.

These earrings might look massive but they were in fact fairly light, as one can tell from the fact that they did not, like the heavy girandoles of the 18th century, require an additional hoop to ease their weight: almost all examples are set with a simple hinged hook fitting into the lobe from back to front.

Typical of English earrings of the time is the widespread use of elongated drops in p. 92, 9 chalcedony or agate (either left white or stained blue or green) and applied with small semiprecious stones such as garnets and turquoises set in gold floral motifs. These earrings usually came with a matching Maltese cross pendant. There are varying degrees of decoration: some are plain drops carved in hardstone, while others show a greater complexity, with applied decoration of naturalistic inspiration. Similarly designed sets set with diamonds are now less common but we know that they existed.

Also popular in England, where diamonds were more plentiful than in France as a consequence of the more stable political and economic situation, were earrings in the form of diamond pear-shaped drops with a large pearl or diamond swing centre on a cluster of foliate surmount.

The simplest form of earring fashionable at the time had a large pear-shaped drop p. 71 of semiprecious stone, usually a faceted amethyst or citrine, mounted in a gold collet suspended from a similarly-set single stone circular or oval surmount.

LONG AND LIGHT EARRINGS

Right: A pair of gold *repoussé* and turquoise pendent earrings, circa 1840. Turquoise and carbuncles in association with gold *repoussé* work were particularly favoured at the time.

Below: A portrait miniature of a lady, by Leopold Grosz (or Gross), circa 1830. Note the fashionable coiffure with hair arranged in three clusters of curls expanding sideways, counterbalanced by cannetille earrings en girandole.

Bottom: Two pairs of *repoussé* gold earrings, circa 1840, one with carbuncle the other with polychrome enamel.

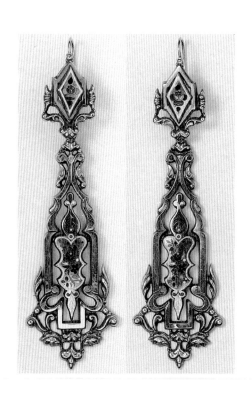

Left and below: Four pairs of pendent earrings, set with citrines and pink topazes, circa 1835, characterized by the combination of cannetille and *repoussé* work which marks the transition between the two goldsmith techniques used in this type of earring.

Typically all the earrings illustrated on these pages are long, light, set with semiprecious gemstones or decorated with polychrome enamels and of moderate intrinsic value.

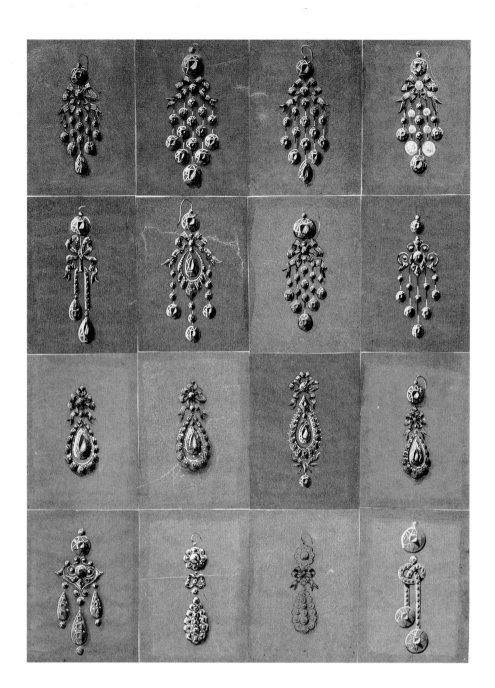

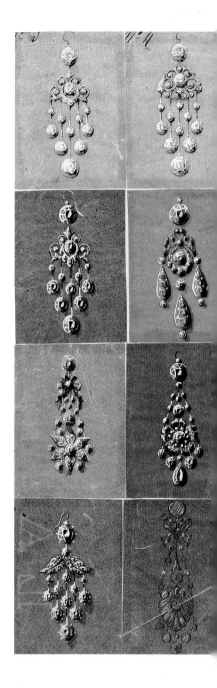

THE 18TH CENTURY REVIVED

Above: Three pages of ink and gouache designs for pendent earrings of the last quarter of the 19th century from the archives of Mellerio, Paris. They include both pendeloques with garlands and fluttering ribbon bows and girandoles in numerous variations, symptomatic of the revival of French 18th-century design especially favoured by the Empress Eugénie. The majority of these earrings were set entirely with diamonds or with a combination of pearls and diamonds. The same stones were favoured for pendent earrings of naturalist inspiration designed as cascades of florets or flowerheads.

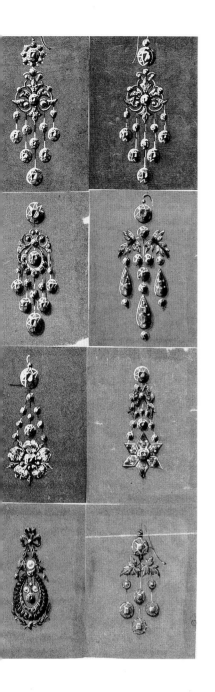

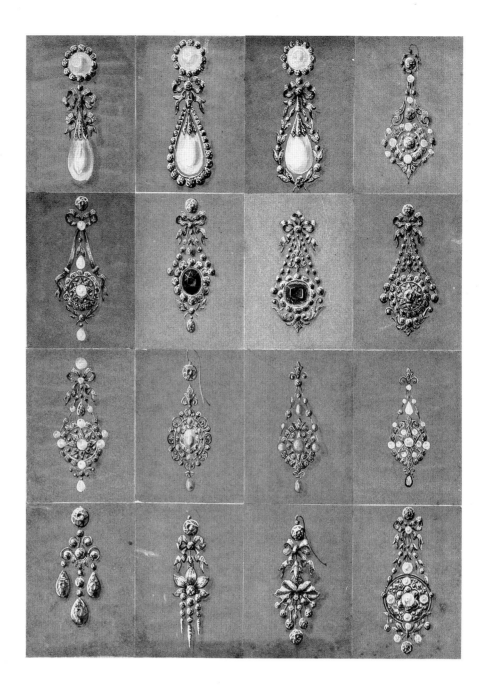

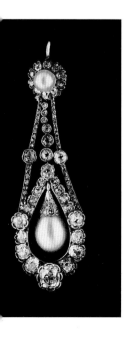

Left: Three pairs of pendent earrings circa 1870–80, English, set with diamonds or pearl and diamonds. The designs, though more rigid and stiff, are close to the contemporary French examples illustrated above, but their fluttering ribbons and garland motifs are replaced by plain lines of diamonds.

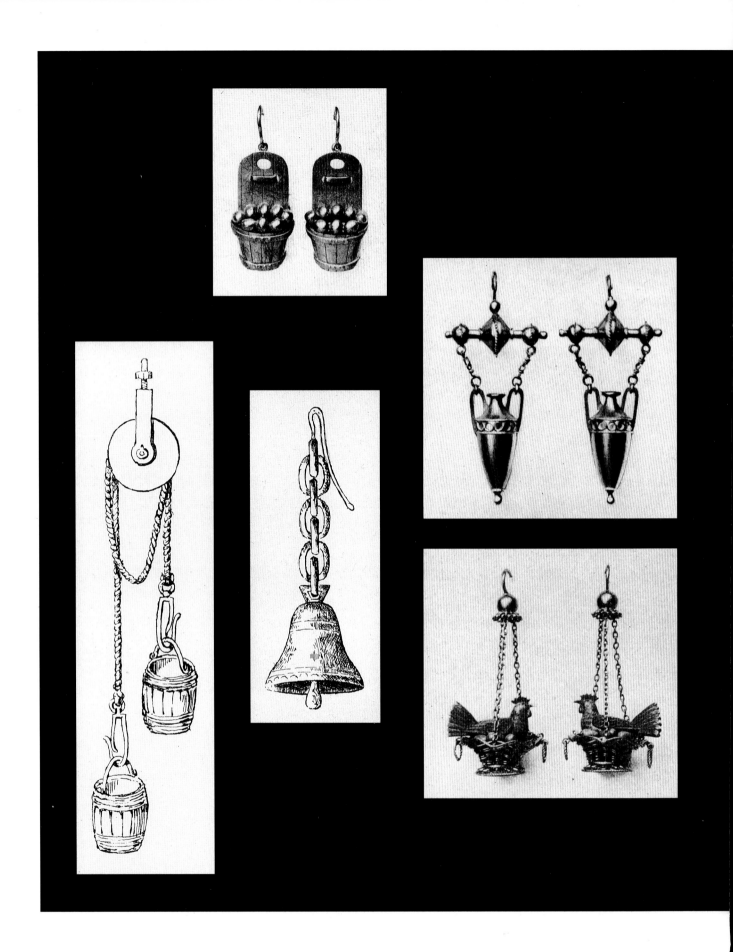

THE 1860s AND 1870s: BIZARRE VARIETY

In the 1860s and 1870s earrings became extremely popular, and the fashionable lady would suspend virtually anything from her ears providing it was decorative. Objects of common use such as baskets of flowers or hammers, animals, natural objects and archaeologically

inspired masks or amphorae were motifs
exploited throughout Europe. So we find an
earring designed as two buckets attached to a
pulley, by Fontenay; French designs in the form
of bells, baskets, hens brooding their eggs and
amphorae; an English earring (illustrated

together with its design by Brogden made in
1867) set with a cameo mask of Dionysos; and
Italian and German earrings in the form of
arrows. In the last example, designed by Kreuter
in 1873, the unusual fitting mechanism gives the
illusion of the arrow actually piercing the lobe.

A parure of emerald, pearl and diamond earrings and matching necklace, with the relevant design, commissioned by Napoleon III and Eugénie from the Parisian jeweller Mellerio in 1863 as a wedding gift to Maréchal Canrobert. The impact of these earrings relies on the use of important gemstones such as the large cabochon emerald drops rather than the explicit archaeological motifs, though the Greek key pattern and the extensive use of yellow gold even for the setting of the diamonds betrays an archaeological interest. Emeralds were the favourite coloured gemstones of the Empress Eugénie and because of this became one of the most popular gemstones of the time.

1840s and 1850s

In the late 1840s a new hairstyle with a parting at the centre and the hair brushed to each side of the face and gathered in a knot at the back, totally covering the ears, led to the virtual disappearance of earrings – another indication of the close relationship between hairstyles and earrings. One has only to look at portraits by Wintherhalter and other society painters to see how universal this fashion was. In the middle of the century Queen Victoria was consistently portrayed with her ears covered, and even in catastrophic situations such as those shown in John Martin's *The Great Day of His Wrath* (1852) or *The Last Judgement* (1853), women in the last extremity of distress are depicted with their ears carefully covered by neatly arranged hair at the sides.

The temporary eclipse of earrings is confirmed by the fact that at the Great Exhibition of 1851 in London, although jewellery was well represented, earrings were not given prominence. Those that were produced at this time were attractive but generally small and compact in design, frequently featuring naturalistic motifs such as flowerhead clusters, bunches of grapes, acorns, and other foliate arrangements chased in gold, set with a gemstone depicting a bud or berry, or carved in coral and ivory. The trend towards naturalism was common to all the decorative arts and jewellery. Other earrings assumed the shape of crescent hoops or elongated beads. Long gem-set earrings were never worn at important formal occasions because the ears remained completely concealed by the hair and covered by elaborate tiaras in the form

p. 120, 121

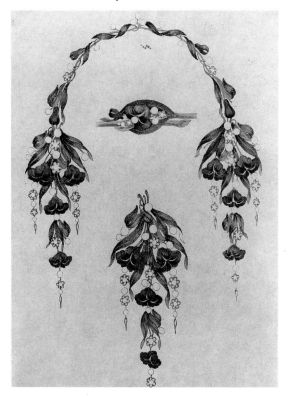

A pencil and gouache design for a tiara, bracelet and corsage ornament by Mellerio, mid 19th century. Note the two lateral cascading spray of leaves and flowers which concealed the ears.

Ink design for a *dormeuse* earring, by Kreuter, Germany, April 1877, front and side view.

of garlands of flowers which framed the face and cascaded in two sprays decorated *en pampille* down the sides of the head. During the day, bonnets with large brims tied under the chin with wide ribbons made earrings superfluous and difficult to wear; for the same reason brooches ceased to be worn high on the collar where they interfered with the hat ribbon tied under the chin. Simple single-stone earrings – know as *dormeuses* or 'sleepers' because they were worn at night to prevent the pierced hole in the lobe from closing – were the only form of earring that continued to be used.

The Exotic: the 1860s and 1870s

In the 1860s hair went up again and earrings returned to favour. Their comeback was marked by a great variety of types and styles. Size fluctuated throughout the period, but grew to enormous proportions in the late 1860s and early 1870s, when earrings almost rested on the shoulder. This fashion, although started in France and England, spread throughout Europe, and we also learn from an article in the trade-paper *Watchmaker, Jeweller and Silversmith* of 1875 that: 'long pendent earrings are coming into fashion again in America.'

It was the great age of novelty. Women suspended from their ears any unusual and bizarre object they could think of. Among the favourite shapes for earring pendants were windmills, buckets, shovels, hammers, hens brooding in baskets, and humming birds. Even exotic creatures such as Brazilian beetles were suspended from ears in the place of gemstones. Goldfish swimming in bowls were simulated by tinted intaglios. The Chinese-inspired 'willow pattern' is seen on many plate-shape gold earrings from 1870, enamelled in blue and white with the traditional pagoda, willow tree and figures on a bridge. Arrow earrings also appear to have been in great favour, either simply attached to the earlobe or designed in two sections so as to appear to transfix it. p. 78

p. 103

p. 79

Earrings of these types were not products of 'haute joaillerie' and not intended to be particularly artistic; they were meant to be amusing and decorative, 'novelty' jewellery to be worn for a season and then discarded. This explains firstly why they are always of little intrinsic value, being made of thin gold leaf decorated with enamel rather than gemstones, and secondly why few of them survive. They were certainly not the type of jewel to pass down in the family as an heirloom.

Interest in travel and advances in scientific knowledge together with the development of new industrial techniques, all affected the design of earrings around the middle of the century. New materials such as 'Blue John' or Derbyshire spar, lava from Vesuvius, colourful feathers of hummingbirds from Mexico, and beetles from Brazil, whose hard and green iridescent shell proved a successful and unusual substitute for gemstones, all made their appearance. The beetles were either simply attached to a gold hook to be inserted through the pierced earlobe or grouped more elaborately in girandole arrangements. There were also exotic flowers, such as cascades of stained ivory fuchsia blossoms; bunches of bulrushes set with turquoises; p. 107, 126

p. 102, 107

p. 104, 106 baskets of flowers held by a hand, and acorns. The popularity of the latter is demonstrated by its appearance among the drawings of Mellerio and by the firm's advertisement in the magazine *La Femme et la Famille et le Journal des Jeunes Personnes*.

p. 102, 103 Animals were also favourite subjects; among the most amusing are frogs ready to spring from bulrushes, nesting birds, brooding hens and coiled serpents entwined with a vine spray. Hammers, ladders and well-pulleys with buckets reflect an interest p. 78 in industry. Although the fashion for novelty earrings appears to have started in France, it assumed its most bizarre forms in England.

Classical revival

Another leitmotiv of 19th-century jewellery is revivalism, a means of enriching the present by looking at the past. This had developed in the 1830s when designers such as Pugin in England and soon after Froment Meurice in France turned to Gothic art as a source of inspiration. Few examples of earrings in Gothic style are known, and those are usually made from Berlin iron, a material particularly well suited to reproducing Gothic tracery. The full bloom of revivalism occurs in the 1860s and 1870s and this is particularly true of jewellery. The styles to be revived were mainly pre-Classical and Classical, Italian and French Renaissance and the period of Louis XVI.

Contemporary archaeological discoveries in Etruria and in the Greek Islands such as Knossos, Melos and Rhodes were bringing to light large quantities of exceptional ancient jewellery. The importance and popularity of earrings in antiquity was in some ways comparable to the 1860s and 1870s. It was natural, therefore, that antique shapes, designs and techniques were copied or reinterpreted in this period.

Among the leaders in this style were the Castellanis in Rome and Naples; they not only copied and reinterpreted the examples of the past but also set antique fragments such as engraved gemstones and coins as part of their interpretation of ancient jewellery. This is particularly evident in works like the gold and cornelian earrings set with Roman intaglios depicting a trophy of arms and a hunting scene.

p. 97 Ernesto Pierret was another famous jeweller in Rome who produced earrings of Etrusco-Roman inspiration. A good example is the pair designed as a triangular panel decorated with bead-work and corded wire typical of Greek and Etruscan goldsmithwork flanked by baton motifs with spherical drop terminals probably inspired by the Roman *crotalia* which Pliny describes as ornaments designed to tinkle at every movement. This was a favourite motif for earrings and many examples survive where the baton-shaped drops are combined with various surmounts such as the Athenian owl with spread wings perched on a pediment.

The taste for Classical designs was widespread throughout Europe. Similar examples were produced by firms such as Robert Phillips in England and Eugène Fonte- p. 109 nay in France. Fontenay made great use of bead-work and corded wire in the mounts of his earrings, which were frequently set with carvings or enamel miniatures of scenes from Pompeian frescoes and had fringed drops and palmette or rosette surmounts.

Gold and pearl earring in archaeological revival style, circa 1870, inspired by the ancient Roman 'crotalia'.

This archaeological fad was such that as early as 1859 it became the target of satirical sketches. In 'A Young Lady on the High Classical School of Ornament', *Punch* (15 July 1859) depicted a devotee of the Antique style with an excess of jewels, tiara, hair ornaments, necklaces, bracelets, pendants and long earrings, all of Greek and Etruscan inspiration.

Some revivalist earrings derive specifically from well known antique prototypes while others are merely pastiches of different archaeological motifs. A good example of the first type is the Etruscan *a baule* earring of 6th/5th century BC pedigree, which p. 101 reappears, almost identical, in the late 1860s. It has one closed side, with a decoration of applied stylized flowerheads, rosettes and wirework typical of ancient examples. The enamel decoration is undoubtedly prompted by close examination of ancient *a baule* earrings, where inlays of glass paste, which unfortunately have barely survived, were used to enliven the decoration. This represents an attempt by the 19th-century jeweller to reproduce in its entirety the ancient prototype and stresses the past importance of polychrome work.

Subjects such as rams' heads, miniature Eros figures riding birds, amphorae of p. 99, 100 various shapes and blackamoors' heads popular in late Classical Greek, Hellenistic and Etruscan earrings were revived in abundance. Not only were the forms derived from Antiquity but also the techniques: granulation was largely used – although never reaching the finesse of Antiquity – with wirework and beading to pick out details, and, as in the past, enamels were preferred to gemstones.

Other popular shapes of Antiquity which had never been related to ear ornaments were now converted into earrings, e.g., Carlo Giuliano's miniature oil lamps decorated with black enamel, modelled on lamps used for votive offerings in temples and sanctuary precincts.

Even 19th-century 'novelty' materials such as lava from Vesuvius, Wedgwood jasper-ware and tortoiseshell were adapted to earrings inspired by the Antique. Somehow the frilliness typical of the 19th century creeps through the severe and linear shapes of archaeological Classicism, so that they could never be mistaken for the real thing. This is particularly true of two pairs of earrings where Roman gold p. 98 low-relief and Greek amphorae are suspended from circular surmounts decorated with frivolous 19th-century flower motifs.

The typical fitting of all these earrings is a thin S-shaped gold hook inserted in the ear from front to back, at times secured, like many ancient examples, by an additional semicircular catch at the back.

Notable as a successful reinterpretation of Classical ideals is the emerald and diamond parure commissioned by Napoleon III from Mellerio; although its overall design is definitely archaeological, its pendent earrings of sober, sculptural shape p. 80 have no strict connection with any ancient prototype.

Besides Greek, Roman and Etruscan art, Egypt provided an important source of inspiration, not only in terms of shapes and designs but also of colour choice and combination. Interest in ancient Egypt was stimulated by the completion of the Suez Canal in 1869 and by the contemporary excavations in the Nile Valley carried out and published by Auguste Mariette. Falcons, papyri, mosaic or gold Pharaoh masks and scarabs were soon fashionable motifs to adorn the ears, and dramatic combinations of bright colours such as lapis or turquoise blue, deep red and opaque white typical of Egyptian art gained favour throughout Europe.

p. 96, 113

Renaissance and 18th-century revival
The Renaissance revival, with its interest in sculptural and figurative shapes and enamel-work, began in the 1840s in France but did not affect earrings until the 1860s and 1870s. Among the influential jewellers working in this style was Carlo Giuliano, an Italian who spent most of his working life in England. Among his most striking works is a pair of earrings in gold and polychrome enamel, opaque and translucent, each in the form of a stork devouring a serpent. In this case not only does the enamel technique and the bold sculptural shape remind us of the famous Renaissance figurative pendants, but the symbolism too is Renaissance; the stork devouring a snake standing for the soul overcoming carnal pleasure derives from a well known Renaissance emblem.

p. 110

Fantastic creatures such as dragons and griffins with pronounced sculptural quality and the widespread use of polychrome enamels were typical of the French Renaissance revival. What gives away the fact that these belong to the 19th and not the 16th century is their passion for ornate and frilly detail, which always tends to creep in and detract from the boldness of the sculptural effect. This is particularly evident in the fringe of pearls and rosette surmount of the griffin earrings reproduced.

p. 111

The gold, polychrome enamel and hardstone cameo earrings, each set with a cameo mask holding a floral festoon suspended from a tree-headed mask surmount, which the London jeweller John Brogden exhibited at the Paris Universal Exhibition of 1867, although imbued with a certain Renaissance feeling, are closer to late 18th-century Neoclassicism. The choice of differently coloured agate for the two cameos of Classical Dionysus masks is a rather unusual feature for the period. It is interesting that in this case both the original design and the finished jewels survive.

p. 79

In France, among other revivals, that of the Louis XVI style was particularly favoured by the Empress Eugénie who, anxious to emulate Marie Antoinette in establishing in France a 'grand' monarchic tradition, revived, together with the crinoline, all the girandoles, bows and ribbon motifs of French 18th-century jewellery. She commissioned J.-E. Bapst, the famous French jeweller, to remount part of the crown jewels in Louis XVI style. The great majority of pendeloque and girandole earrings revived at this time in France were set with pearls and diamonds, but Eugénie's favourite stone was the emerald, and it quickly became the most popular coloured gemstone in France.

p. 74, 77

85

Fin de siècle

As a consequence of the opening up of Japan to trade with Europe in the 1850s and of the revolution there in 1866, Japanese art, until then little known in the West, started to exert considerable influence on the evolution of ornament and decoration. In the mid-1870s it became popular in Europe to mount small pieces of Japanese metalwork as jewellery. Shakudo and shibuichi, the metal inlay techniques developed by Samurai swordmakers for the decoration of sword mounts and guards, entered the world of jewellery. Shibuichi and shakudo plaques and miniature fans decorated with flowers, butterflies, insects, birds and bamboo provided with a small suspension hook became very fashionable earrings and the Europeans soon began to imitate them in chased gold and silver. A good example is the pair of pendent earrings in the shape of a rectangular plaque decorated with fan-shaped motifs. p. 101

The increasing ease of travel in Europe encouraged interest in foreign countries and people liked to bring home souvenirs of the localities they visited. Italy with its sights and monuments was amongst the favourite destinations. Souvenir earrings are usually made of materials which are typical of a certain location: Roman mosaics, or p. 112, 113 micromosaic, made of minute glass tesserae depicting sights of Rome or scenes from the Campagna, and Florentine mosaic made of larger pieces of variously coloured inlaid semiprecious hardstone, usually in floral patterns, were extremely popular. Roman and Florentine mosaics had in fact been used in jewellery since the early 1800s; the earliest form of mosaic earrings consisted of a simple oval plaque con- p. 114 nected to a smaller panel surmount with fine gold chains. Later examples dating from p. 98, 115 the 1860s and 1870s are much more varied in shape and often reminiscent of archaeological revival designs. Early examples of Roman mosaic earrings have almost unbelievably tiny glass tesserae, producing a precision of detail which matches that of painting. Later examples are much coarser.

Among the plethora of 1860s and 1870s earrings another type can be clearly distinguished, known as the 'fringe' earring. This usually consists of a circular or oval p. 122, 123 surmount above a fringe of articulated pointed drops. It was popular throughout Europe but especially fashionable in England around 1870 where the drops tight-

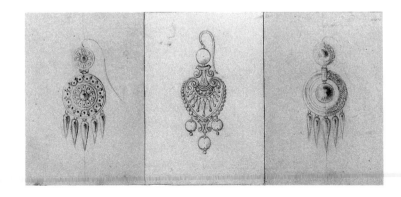

Three earring designs in pencil and gouache of the late 1870s, from the archives of Mellerio, Paris. Note the fringe ornament typical of the time.

ened up to form a compact fringe of tapered gold chains in contrast to their Continental counterparts where the pendent elements are frequently fewer and well spaced. The distinction is clear if one compares the French designs illustrated in Mellerio's archives with English examples set with carbuncles, Wedgwood jasperware plaques or decorated with white and royal blue or turquoise coloured enamel. The inset of small pearls or diamonds in a starshaped motif at the centre of the gemstone or enamelled boss surmount is another typical feature of jewellery of the time. Archaeological influence is frequently noticeable on the surmounts of these earrings. Most examples are fairly voluminous and long, measuring approximately 6 to 10 cms; in spite of this, their weight is negligible since the fringes that constitute a large portion of the earring are made of hollow gold drops or of light gold chain. More expensive examples of diamond-set fringe earrings, though less common, are well known.

p. 123

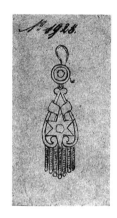

p. 116

Naturalism in jewellery reached its peak in this period under the spell of the Parisian Oscar Massin, whose naturalistic and botanically accurate creations characterized by *tremblant* and *pampille* decoration became a model for jewellers throughout Europe. Cascades of flowerheads, sprays of leaves and flowers and single flowerhead clusters were to be seen on grand occasions. The designs by Mellerio and by the German Frederich Kreuter reproduced here illustrate the variety of forms fashionable at the time.

p. 124, 125

The star motif had been popular in jewellery since the 1860s. At first its design was exploited mainly for brooches, and only in the late 1860s was it introduced into earring design. Typical of this date are earrings mounted with large carbuncles, amethyst cabochons or enamelled gold bosses inlaid at the centre with a pearl or diamond star-shaped motif. In other examples the whole earring takes on the shape of a star suspended by a simple hook from the ear. The basic six-pointed star offered scope for many variations: the points could multiply up to eighteen, of different lengths and widths. In the late 1880s and 1890s knife-wire settings came into favour and this, together with a taste for light and less symmetrical shapes, prompted the creation of elaborate earrings in the form of off-centre stars, comets and shooting stars. The favourite gemstones for this type of ornament were diamonds since they could best suggest real stars; less expensive versions were set with half pearls and very pale opals. Many sets were made in this style, comprising earrings, a brooch, and a necklace which could also be worn as a tiara; a design by Mellerio commissioned by Queen Isabella II of Spain is a good example.

p. 116, 117

Towards the end of the century the fashion for large and varied earrings subsided in favour of smaller and more sober ear ornaments, either clusters or single gemstones, simply claw- or collet-set in very unobtrusive, delicate mounts provided at the back with a flattened hoop fitting. The fashionable design for daywear in the 1890s consisted simply of a single pearl embellished with small diamonds. At night the favourite earring would be a single diamond of varying size. The change towards smaller earrings was this time dictated not so much by hairstyles, since the ears were

Four ink designs for pendent earrings by Kreuter, Germany, 1867–70. The top one is star shaped; the second and fourth decorated with star and fringe motifs; and the third with a fringe only.

p. 128

A collection of North Italian gold pendent earrings, circa 1800. Their large size, linearity and two-dimensional, geometrical quality are typical of early 19th-century earrings in Europe. Many include a central plaque in relief stamped out of a thin sheet of gold, to simulate a cameo with a profile of a Classical warrior, a type of imagery which had become popular at the time of the Napoleonic campaign in Northern Italy of 1796–97. Note the contrast between the austere profiles and the delicate lace-like filigree border decorated with typical hollow hemispherical motifs.

still left uncovered, as by the fashion for high frilled collars during the day and for the '*collier de chien*', or dog collar, at night, both of which dressed the neck and filled in the space between ears and shoulders. Long pendent earrings which visually interfered with high collars and neck ornaments disappeared almost completely. The few pendent earrings of the 1890s were of moderate size, in the shape of very delicate pearl and diamond articulated drops which moved and reflected light.

The discovery of the Cape diamond mines in South Africa brought a plentiful supply of fine stones onto the market. A single, large, flawless, white diamond of high quality was now usually preferred to a fussy arrangement of small stones. The new abundance of diamonds also led to new ways of cutting: cushion-shaped diamonds, fat and bulky in order to retain the maximum carat weight of precious material, became thinner and circular in shape, with the culet or back facet reduced to a pin-point, thus exploiting to the maximum the exceptional optical quality of diamonds to reflect and disperse light. The new brilliant cut involved a waste of up to 50% of the rough crystal but the final result was thought to be worth it.

Apart from diamonds, a variety of other stones were set in cluster earrings; often a larger coloured stone would be mounted within a border of smaller diamonds. Opals, together with pale and metallic sapphires from Montana, appeared on the market in the 1890s; amethysts and peridots were great favourites and with their purple and lime green colours well complemented the pastel tints of contemporary dresses. In the 1890s pearls and half-pearls were the preferred alternative to the more expensive diamond borders and with their delicate sheen particularly suited the soft silks in fashion during the last decade of the century.

The Art Nouveau movement, which reacted against the repetitiveness and lack of imagination in the decorative arts and jewellery and challenged the excessive emphasis placed on intrinsic value, promoted many new, original and daring designs – but not for earrings. There are hardly any Art Nouveau earrings, and the few that survive must be considered exceptions. An extraordinary pair created by René Lalique is definitely a 'one off'. They are typical in their choice of less expensive materials (large milky opals, translucent enamels echoing the colour of the opals, richly coloured matt gold) and in the flowing line of the decorative thistle motif rendered in enamel at the front and engraved at the back. But they are unique in their unconventionally large size and their detachable clip fitting, a feature which became normal only in the 1930s. It is possible that such clip fittings were devised to allow the earrings to be worn as necklace pendants.

WAFER-THIN: EARRINGS OF THE EARLY 19TH CENTURY

Right: A portrait of Maria de la Conception Rodriguez of Granada, painted by José Gil in 1816. Her earrings, typical of the early 19th century, are two circular gold plaques set with corals connected by fine chains. Their linearity and two-dimensional quality is well suited to the low décolleté and contemporary hairstyle of Classical inspiration.

Above left: A diamond pendent earring, early 19th century, showing how the structure of the contemporary gold earrings made of articulated plaques was rendered, almost unaltered, in lavish gemstones such as diamonds.

Above right: Pair of gold earrings, early 19th century, made of several paper-thin gold plaques of different shapes connected by lateral chains.

Above left: Pair of gold earrings, early 19th
century. Although quite long, these earrings are
comfortable to wear because they are cut out of
very thin and light gold sheet and not set with
gemstones.

Above right: A pair of gold and enamel pendent
earrings, probably French, early 19th century,
decorated with portrait miniatures of a man and
his wife. Though the design is typical of the
time, this pair presents unusual sentimental
imagery: a dove, a pair of flaming hearts, the
inscription 'Fidel' and forget-me-nots.

TORPEDO-SHAPED DROPS OF THE
1830s AND 1840s

Opposite and below: Three pairs of gold, chalcedony and gem-set pendent earrings, each accompanied by a typical Maltese cross pendant en suite, circa 1830. Contemporary fashion encouraged the use of such elongated drops decorated with applied gold floral motifs, often set with turquoises or other coloured gemstones. They were carved in white or stained chalcedony, usually blue or green.

Right and far right: Two examples of *repoussé* gold earrings of elongated drop design, circa 1840, the first applied with turquoise florets, the second decorated with quatrefoil motifs suspended from a shell-shaped surmount. Earrings of this type were usually made of thin foils of metal decorated *en repoussé* and extremely long (10–12 cms). Their size and lightness were dictated by fashion and economic factors. The exaggerated horizontal lines of dress and hairstyle needed to be offset by long pendants, while at the same time the scarcity of precious metal encouraged the use of wafer-thin foil of embossed gold.

Below centre: A gold and gem-set torpedo-shaped earring, circa 1835, combining embossed and cannetille decoration.

1830s:
FROM CANNETILLE TO REPOUSSÉ

Left: Two gold, cannetille diamond and gem-set
parures, English, circa 1830. In both cases the
parures include a pair of earrings set with rubies
and emeralds respectively. Though the design is
that of the traditional girandole, the setting in
cannetille is typical of the time, the design of the
earrings matching those of the necklace
pendants. On the Continent canetille earrings
were mainly set with semiprecious stones such as
foiled topazes, amethysts and citrines. In
England more expensive gemstones such as
emeralds, diamonds and rubies were often used.

Right: An exceptional pair of pendent earrings
set with aquamarines within *repoussé* gold
borders, circa 1835. These earrings are typical
of the time for their length (12 cms
approximately), for their lightness (15 grams)
and for the choice of the stones, two large kite-
shaped aquamarines. The lightness of the mount
makes them comfortable to wear in spite of their
size. Gold *repoussé* work replaced cannetille
because it was cheaper to manufacture and used
small quantities of precious metal.

EGYPTIAN AND CLASSICAL STYLE

Above: An impressive pair of gold earrings and matching necklace, circa 1870. The dominating element of these jewels is the pharaoh mask, so the Egyptian inspiration is sufficiently obvious. Nonetheless the surmount is Classical Greek, a rosette; 19th-century revivalism was often the result of such combination of elements deriving from different cultures and periods.

Opposite:
A group of Classical revival earrings, circa 1865. *Top left:* laurel leaf suspended from an Athenian owl surmount. *Top right:* A pair of gold rams' head earrings, deriving its design from Greek examples of the late Classical period, the antique counterparts usually consist of a tapered hoop to be inserted into the earlobe terminating with a rams' head motif, in this case the rams' head is suspended from a rosette surmount. *Below left:* A pair of gold and cornelian intaglio earrings, by Castellani, incorporating original Roman intaglios that depict a trophy of arms and a hunting scene. *Below right:* A pair of gold pendent earrings, by Ernesto Pierret, each designed as a triangular panel decorated with beaded work and corded wire typical of Greek and Etruscan goldsmithwork, flanked by baton motifs with spherical drop terminals.

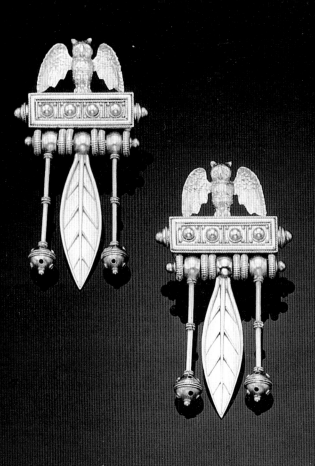

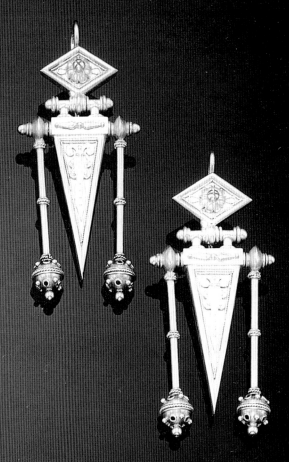

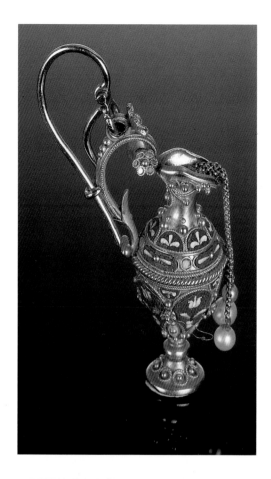

Opposite: Two pairs of Roman earrings, circa 1870. The first by Civilotti of Rome, combines elements from various sources. The amphora motifs in matt gold find precise counterparts in Greek and Etruscan examples, the gold mosaic plaque with its Christian symbolism is reminiscent of Byzantine mosaics, while the lilies of the circular surmounts belong unmistakably to the 19th century. The second pair, of gold and Roman mosaic, carry lozenge-shaped plaques with portraits of Sabina and Maximus Caesar. Note in this case the contrast between the sober, classical lines of the pendant and the frivolous design of the floral surmount.

Above: A pair of gold and enamel pendent earrings, circa 1870, in the shape of stylized amphorae. The design has no specific counterpart in Antiquity but is a pastiche of various elements. The amphora motif derives from a popular type of Hellenistic earring; the granulation and corded wire decoration from Greek and Etruscan tradition; and the stylized papyri and palmettes in bright contrasting colours are Egyptian.

Left: A pair of gold and Roman mosaic earrings, circa 1870, in the shape of ewers. The gold chains with pearl terminals are meant to simulate water being poured out – an amusing 19th-century touch not to be found in Antiquity.

A RANGE OF REVIVALS: THE 1870s

Many Classical designs took the amphora as their model, in, for instance, tortoiseshell (*right*) or lapis lazuli (*below right*). Rams' heads feature as a pair of gold earrings (*below*).

Above: Gold and enamel *a baule* earrings in the Etruscan tradition, seen in front, back and side views. *Right top left to bottom right:* Hardstone maenad heads set in elaborate gold and enamel mounts; gold rosette; Wedgwood jasper-ware drops decorated with a white figurative frieze on a blue ground; two earrings based on amphorae in matt gold; and finally a pair of Japanese-influenced gold and polychrome enamel earrings designed as fans on screens.

LIGHTHEARTED EARRINGS OF
THE 1860s AND 1870s

Common features of these earrings are a playful
naturalistic inspiration, the use of relatively
inexpensive material such as gold, enamel, ivory
and turquoises, and the combination of bright
colours. They are in line with the concept of
novelty jewellery, more a fashion accessory –
hence the low value of the materials – than
precious heirlooms to be treasured.

Left-hand column
Above: A pair of gold and turquoise pendent
earrings in the shape of bulrush sprays, the
heads pavé-set with turquoises. English, circa
1860.
Below: A pair of gold and enamel earrings,
French, circa 1870, designed as birds nesting in
bulrushes.

Centre column
Above: A pair of gold and tinted intaglio
earrings, English, circa 1870, depicting
goldfish in round bowls.

Middle: A pair of three-coloured gold and
enamel earrings, probably French, circa 1860,
designed as coiled snakes supporting bunches of
grapes.

Below: A pair of gold and enamel earrings,
English, circa 1870, in the form of frogs
amongst bulrushes in a triangular frame of
twigs.

Right-hand column
Above: A pair of gold and tinted ivory earrings,
English, circa 1860, designed as cascades of
fuchsia blossom carved in tinted pink ivory.

Below: A pair of silver-gilt and turquoise
earrings in the form of nesting birds pavé-set
with turquoises, the wire-work nests containing
pearl eggs, French, 1850–60.

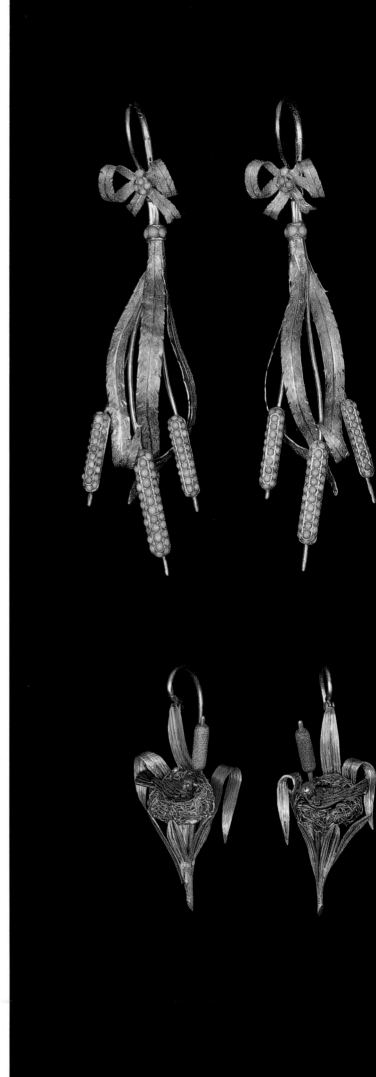

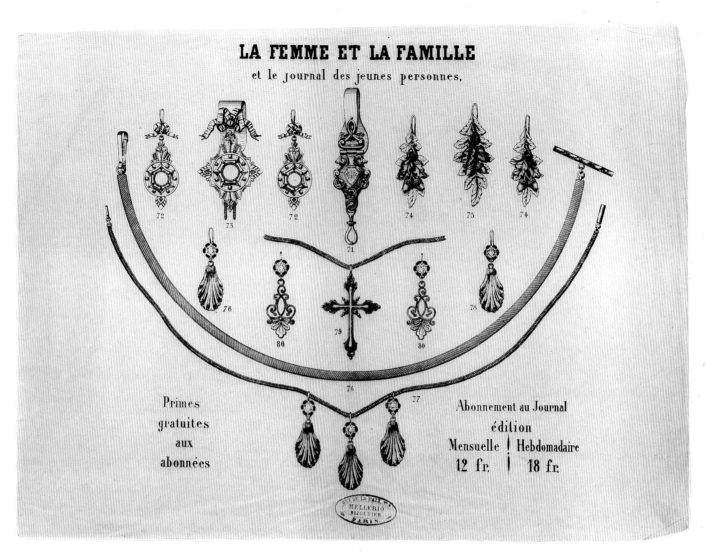

LA FEMME ET LA FAMILLE

et le Journal des jeunes personnes,

72 73 72 71 74 75 74

78 80 79 80 78

76 77

Primes
gratuites
aux
abonnées

Abonnement au Journal
édition
Mensuelle | Hebdomadaire
12 fr. | 18 fr.

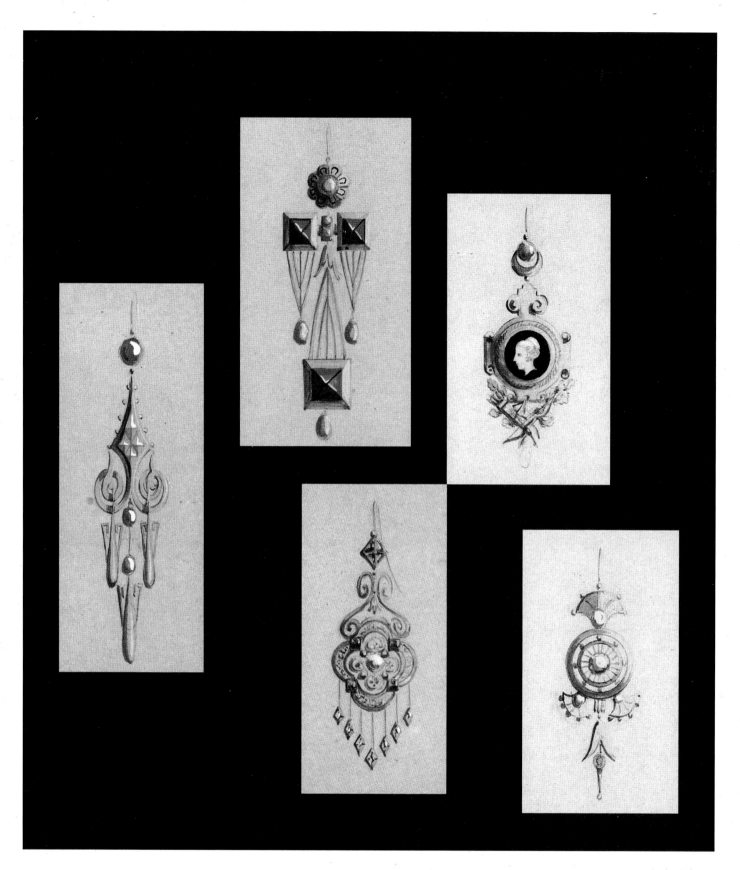

FASHIONS OF THE 1870s

Above: Five designs for earrings from the archives of Mellerio, Paris. Their variety is a reflection of the eclecticism of contemporary jewellery design. Noticeable, however, is the persistence of motifs of archaeological inspiration such as the amphora-shaped drops, the cameo supporting a trophy of love and stylized papyri.

Opposite: Among the earrings of naturalistic inspiration fashionable in the 1870s, those designed as acorns found great favour throughout Europe. In Mellerio's archive are two variations of the same design (*below*), while similar earrings with a matching pendant are advertised in a contemporary issue of the magazine *La Femme et la Famille*.

Right: Stylized papyri also form the surmount of this English gold and turquoise earring.

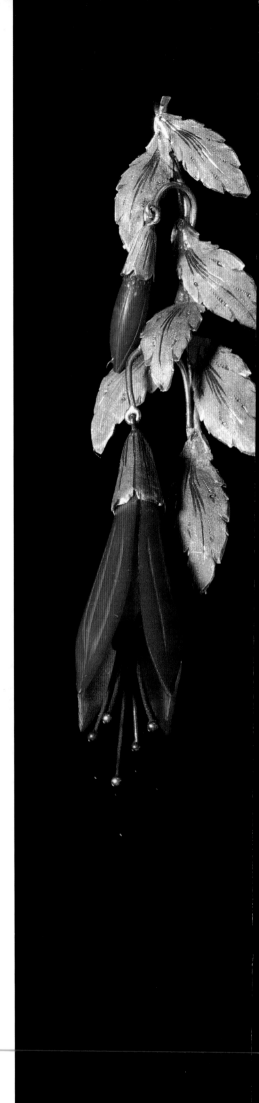

RETURN TO NATURE

During the 1860s women suspended all sorts of ornaments from their ears, from delicate and appealing bouquets of flowers to rather repulsive Brazilian beetles.

Far left: Two pairs of Italian gold earrings, 1860s. The upper pair, set with pearls, has rather disturbing hands supporting a basket of flowers. The lower pair consists of acorns on a two-oak-leaves surmount.

Left: A pair of gold and stained ivory earrings designed as cascading fuchsia blossoms, English, 1860s.

Above: A pair of Brazilian beetle earrings, English, 1860s. The improved communication with South America prompted the introduction of unusual materials such as Brazilian beetles, whose hard, brilliant and iridescent green shell could be mounted as a gemstone.

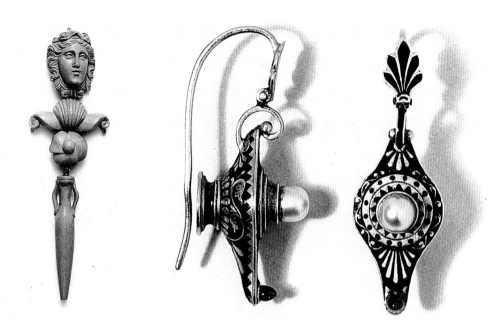

EROS, AMPHORAE AND OIL LAMPS

Variations of amphora- and lamp-shaped earrings, circa 1870. *Left:* A mask of a Maenad supports an amphora carved in lava from Vesuvius, and a pair of gold, enamel and pearl earrings in the shape of oil lamps, by Carlo Giuliano, circa 1865, modelled on lamps used for votive offerings. *Below:* a pair of gold earrings designed as amphorae suspended from fine chains; a gold ewer-shaped earring decorated with corded wire and granulation; and a seed pearl, gold and banded agate earring designed as an amphora on a disc surmount, by Carlo Giuliano, bearing the maker's mark C.G. and the retailer's mark HR for Hunt and Roskell of London.

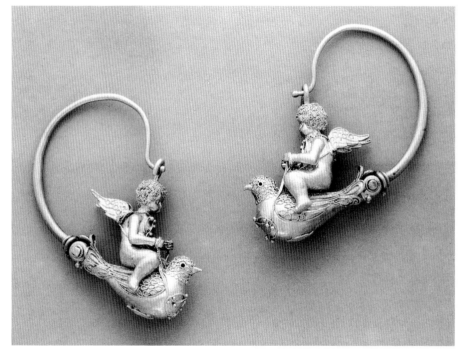

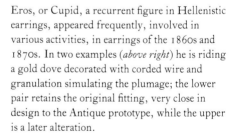

Eros, or Cupid, a recurrent figure in Hellenistic earrings, appeared frequently, involved in various activities, in earrings of the 1860s and 1870s. In two examples (*above right*) he is riding a gold dove decorated with corded wire and granulation simulating the plumage; the lower pair retains the original fitting, very close in design to the Antique prototype, while the upper is a later alteration.

In a pair of gold and enamel pendent earrings by Eugène Fontenay, circa 1870 (*above*), Eros is depicted carrying wine jugs on painted enamel plaques imitating Roman wall paintings, while in a pair of gold, seed pearl and enamel earrings by Carlo Giuliano, last quarter of the 19th century (*bottom right*) he is playing the lyre and holding a mirror, on circular enamelled plaques.

Left and far left: Two pairs of earrings set with cameos carved respectively in lava and banded agate, circa 1870.

RENAISSANCE REVIVAL

A pair of gold and polychrome earrings, by
Carlo Giuliano, circa 1865, designed as a stork
devouring a snake. The subject derives from a
Renaissance emblem – the soul overcoming
carnal pleasures – and the interest in the
sculptural effect from Renaissance jewellery.

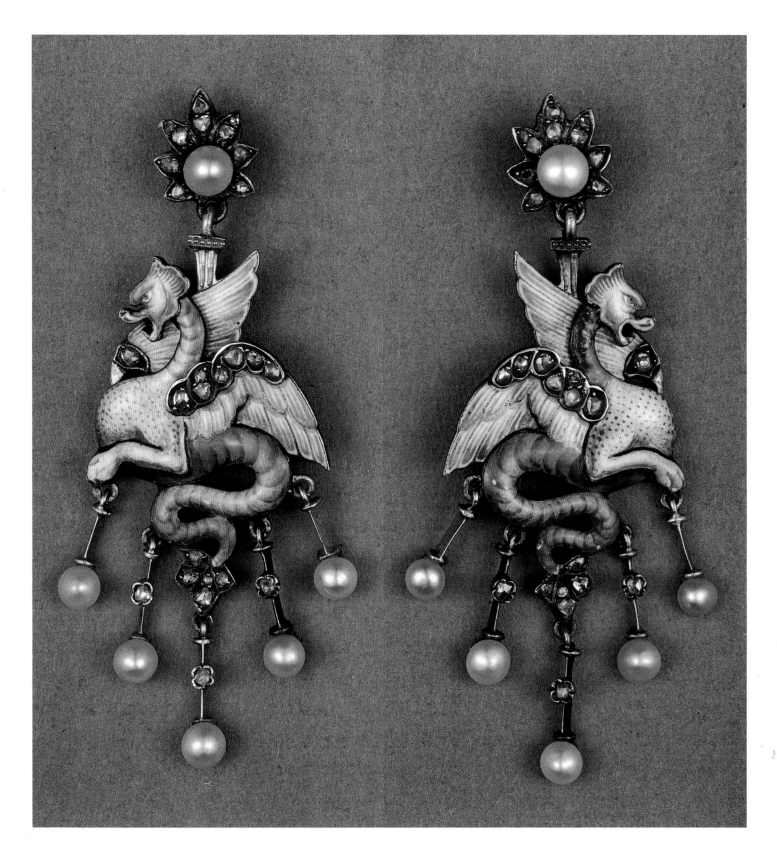

A pair of gold, polychrome enamel and pearl earrings, French, circa 1865. The sculptural quality, the extensive use of enamel and the choice of the subject is reminiscent of Renaissance jewellery, tempered however by the typically 19th-century fringe motifs and rosette surmounts.

Above: A pair of gold and Roman mosaic earrings and matching brooch/pendant, the surmounts of the earrings depicting red, green and white scarabs supporting three elongated drops.

Left: A gold and Roman mosaic pendent earring, the circular surmount decorated with a dolphin and supporting an elaborate drop decorated with the figure of Cupid.

ROMAN AND FLORENTINE MOSAICS OF THE 1870s

Roman and Florentine mosaics, widely exploited in jewellery at the beginning of the 19th century, came back in great favour in the late 1860s. Roman micromosaic technique was especially favoured, not only because it was suited to render motifs of archaeological inspiration but also because its technique derived from Antiquity. This consisted in arranging minute coloured glass paste tessarae within hardstone, glass or gold borders.

Left: Gold earrings of archaeological design decorated with Roman mosaic plaques of winged putti, and a brooch/pendant showing a Raphael tondo.

Below left: A pair of Florentine mosaic earrings set with onyx and coloured stones. Florentine mosaic consisted of an inlay of differently coloured hard and semiprecious stones arranged in naturalistic patterns.

Below centre: A pair of gold and Roman mosaic half-hoop earrings in Egyptian revival style. Note the scarab, similar to the example illustrated on the opposite page.

Below right: A Roman mosaic earring of floral design.

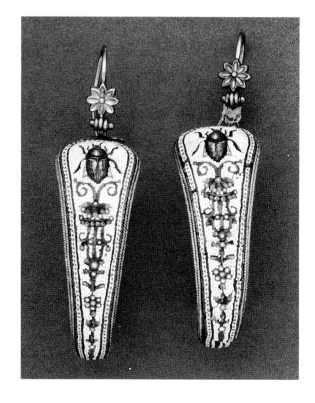

SOUVENIR EARRINGS

Since the beginning of the century
earrings and other jewels set with Roman
mosaic plaques depicting architectural
views of Rome or scenes from the
Campagna had been popular souvenirs to
take back home. Early 19th-century
earrings are characterized by a very
simple and linear design. They usually
consist of an oval surmount supporting a
pear-shaped drop or an oval plaque
connected by fine chains. The mosaics are
of a high quality, consisting of very small
tessarae where the colours are graduated
in a very subtle manner giving the
illusion of a miniature painting. A good
example of this is the pair of earrings
(*left*) set with four mosaic plaques of
famous views of Rome including the
Pyramid of Cestius and the Columns of
Trajan and Antoninus.

Later examples of the 1860s and 1870s
tend to be more elaborate in design,
adapting shapes and decorations to
contemporary trends. The quality of the
mosaics though, is coarser, a consequence
of the increased demand. The earrings
and matching pendant (*right*) with mosaic
plaques depicting peasant women of the
Campagna in the typical *ciociara* costume
are good examples of the time; their
Roman origin is confirmed by the city's
gold hallmark. Note the ubiquitous
Egyptian scarab motif on the surmount
and the coarse tessarae.

Star motifs first appeared in the late 1860s as an inlaid central decorative motif of earrings set with large cabochon gemstones such as amethysts and carbuncles or enamel bosses as the example illustrated here in black enamel and half pearls (*far left*). Later six-, eight-, twelve-pointed stars, or more, became extremely popular, often accompanied by a matching pendant and set for instance, with pearls (*left*).

The popularity of knife-wire setting and the fashion for light and less symmetrical shapes prompted, in the late 1880s and 1890s, the development of shooting stars and comets.

Opposite centre and far left below:
Numerous points alternate with weightless knife-wires set with diamonds. *Left:* A pear-shaped drop terminating with a graduated fringe. *Above:* Set of twelve-pointed star earrings and matching pendant set with pale opals.

Top right: Designs by Mellerio for two variations of star-shaped pendent earrings, part of a parure commissioned by Queen Isabella II of Spain.

INNOVATION AND TRADITION:
FRENCH EARRINGS OF THE 1870s AND 1880s

Two pages of earring designs in pencil and gouache of the late 1870s and early 1880s from the archives of Mellerio, Paris. They range from naturalistic floral creations to pendeloques and girandoles in the 18th-century tradition, mainly set with pearls and diamonds, together with amusing arrows which appear to pierce the ear, in the style of novelty jewellery. The eclecticism of the sources of inspiration is especially evident on the right-hand page, where Classical archaeology with a typical Greek key pattern, naturalism with floral motifs, Persian and Northern African art with boteh and crescent hoops co-exist.

1874

Mars	22	328	Occasion	1 d. fleurette turquoise + roses	75	"	74 Juin	1
Avril	7	329	Bureau	2 d. violette avec roses p.	48	"	74 9bre	2
"	"	330	"	1 " " sans roses	20	"	74 Juin	1
"	10	331	"	1 d. bleuets entrouverts	45	"	76 Juillet	12
"	"	332	Catin	1 d. églantine			74 Juin	1
				émaillé rose + blanc	75	"	"	11
"	"	333	Anzendrin	1 dre or de couleur ciselé			1876	
				repercé + perles	130	"	9bre	2
"	"	6		1 dre or rouge p poli			"	"
"	14	334		gravure griffons			74 xbre	28
				Mont 80, gravure + ciis 20	100	"	74 Juin	30
				1 dre en émaux monture			1878	4
"	"	335	Vincent	or rouge repercé à graver			8bre	"
				monture 70 émail + ciis 20	90	"	"	18
"	15	336	Spire	1 d. bouton d'or	45	"	74 avril	15
"	16	337	Catin	1 d. églantine émaillé bleu + blanc	42	"	74 Mai	21
"	17	338	Spire	1 d. boutons d'or	45	"	"	28
"	24	339	Gex	1 dre repercé or rouge			74 xbre	14
				émail peint 20, mont 130 ciis 5	155	"	"	4
"	25	340	Catin	1 dre boutons marguerite			Juin	4
				paquerette émaillé blanc + bleu	42	"	"	"
Mai	7	341	Anzendrin	1 dre pend repercé			Mai	30
				avec turquoise + perles	105		"	"
		342	Occasion	1 dre joaillerie argent	250	"	Juin	4
				cire roses sur cristal				
				bleu				

Above: A collection of gold and gem-set earrings spanning the years from 1850 to the 1870s. Noticeable are the small compact earrings of the 1850s designed as clusters of foliate motifs or coiled ribbons; the long pointed drops of the 1860s in archaeological revival style; the oval panels star-set with half pearls of the early 1870s, and the tiger's claw earrings fringed by gold drops of the 1870s, brought back from India as souvenirs to commemorate hunting expeditions.

Left: A page of earring drawings from Cartier's archive in Paris, dated from March 1874 to May 1874, illustrating some of the great number of shapes, both long and short, fashionable at the time.

ENDLESS INVENTION

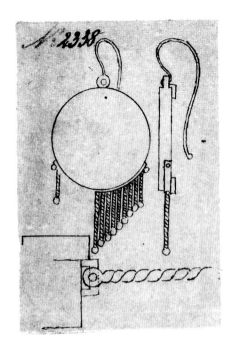

FRINGED EARRINGS OF THE 1870s

One of the most distinctive forms of earring in the 1870s consisted of a circular, oval or otherwise shaped panel variously decorated with enamel, gemstones or chased gold, supporting a graduated fringe of articulated pointed drops. The type was particularly fashionable in England where the favourite surmounts for the tagged drops were oval carbuncles (*below*), or enamel plaques star-set at the centre with various gemstones (*opposite*). Fringe or tassel earrings with matching pendants were popular throughout Europe as testified by the archival records of the German jeweller Kreuter dating from 1868 to 1872 (*right*). More unusual surmounts were occasionally exploited, such as the trapeze-shaped Wedgwood jasper-ware plaque (*opposite lower right*).

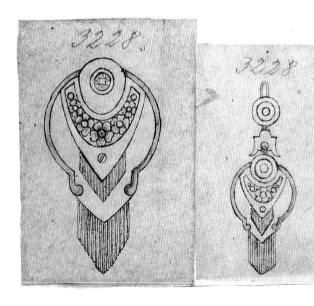

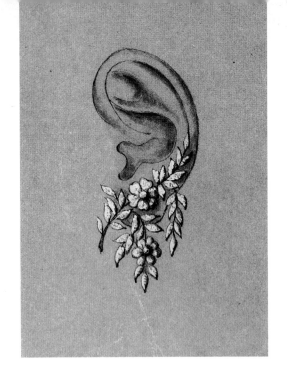

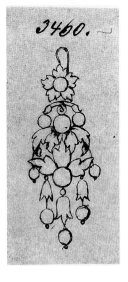

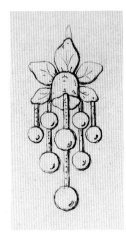

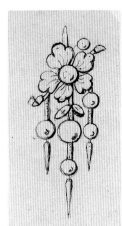

CASCADES OF FLOWERS

Among the plethora of 1870s earrings those designed as cascades of flowers, flowerhead clusters with *pampille* decorations or sprays of leaves and flowers were particularly favoured by a more conservative public.

Far left, top: A pencil and gouache drawing by Mellerio depicting a flower spray earring. It is interesting to note how the design includes the ear to show precisely how the earring should be positioned on it. Beneath it are two ink designs by Mellerio in the form of flowers with cascading stamens.

Left: Two ink drawings by the German jeweller Kreuter of 1873, depicting earrings in the shape of cascades of flowerheads and leaves.

Lower left: A gold and turquoise demi-parure comprising a pair of fuchsia earrings and a matching pendant. Note the naturalistic rendering of the blossoms and the use of *calibré*-cut turquoises. Though turquoise had been a popular stone for many decades it is only in the 1870s that it began to be cut *en calibré* in order to fit the shape of the mount.

Opposite: English diamond-set examples belonging to the same type as those by Kreuter.

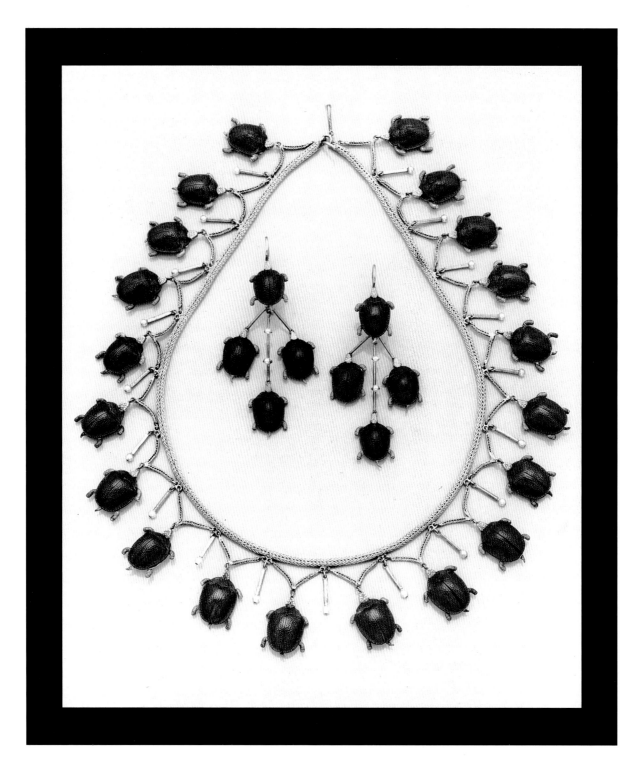

BEETLES AND BACCHUS

A gold and Brazilian beetle demi-parure comprising a
necklace and a pair of pendent earrings of modified
girandole design, probably English, circa 1870. In this
case a 'novelty' material – the Brazilian beetles – is
combined with an overall archaeological design in a
bizarre and unconventional way. The iridescent green
beetles are turned into miniature tortoises by the
addition of feet, head and tail in gold; on the earrings
they are clustered in groups of four.

A gold and seed pearl demi-parure, circa 1865. Vine
leaves and clusters of grapes had been popular in
jewellery since the mid-19th century but their
association with Dionysiac cults made them a favourite
subject for archaeologically inspired creations. In this
case, the Dionysiac imagery is continued in the form of
a thyrsus brooch surmount; the geometric arrangement
of the fringe necklace and its baton-shaped linking are
typical of archaeological revival jewellery.

ARTISTRY OF LALIQUE

Right: A pair of opal, enamel and gold pendent earrings, by René Lalique, French, circa 1900, in their original case. The fluid line, the thistle motif, the choice of the opal as a gemstone and the opalescent enamel epitomizes Art Nouveau jewellery. Though earrings continued to be worn at this time, they were not a particularly prominent ornament so the large proportions of this pair of Lalique earrings are an exception rather than the rule. Even within Lalique's unconventional and daring production of jewellery, they may be regarded as a rarity. The back view (*bottom*) shows the unusual clip fitting which anticipates the fashionable clips of the thirties.

Upper left: A collection of very simple and relatively small earrings typical of late 19th century and of the very beginning of the 20th century. From left to right: A peridot and diamond cluster earring, the large peridot claw-set at the centre; a diamond earring simply claw set with a brilliant-cut stone; a carbuncle (cabochon almandine garnet) and rose diamond cluster earring, probably by Boucheron; a diamond earring designed as a circular cluster of table-cut stones.

4

Experiment and variety: earrings of today

In the first years of the 20th century dress fashions did not change drastically, and cluster and small pendent earrings characteristic of the last decade of the 19th century continued to be popular. The few drop earrings produced were of moderate size and in 'garland' style, that is, characterized by very delicate garland and fluttering bow motifs, usually mounted with diamonds in millegrain settings. The source of inspiration lay in 18th-century France, especially decorative and architectural details such as ormolu furniture fittings and cornices and stucco mouldings. Cartier in particular encouraged his designers to wander through the streets of Paris studying and sketching architectural details. Typical of earrings in this style was the pear-shaped drop, with a coloured gemstone or a diamond briolette, mounted as a swing centre within a garland of small, delicate leaf and flower motifs on a ribbon bow surmount. Other fashionable earrings assumed the form of diamond or coloured stone briolettes on fine articulated chains of millegrain-set diamonds.

Before the First World War
The delicacy of these jewels was enhanced by extensive use of platinum, a white, untarnishable precious metal which was heavy, hard to work and difficult to solder but of great structural strength so that only a little of it was required to produce a sturdy mount.

The desire to set diamonds in a mount whose colour did not alter their whiteness had been felt as early as the 18th century, and since then the traditional metal for diamond setting had been silver. The relative softness of silver, though, required a large amount of metal for the mount and had the great disadvantage of staining the skin and clothing. To overcome the problem, 19th-century jewellers devised a new kind of setting consisting of a laminate of silver and gold: silver at the front so as to set off the colour of the stone to best effect, and gold at the back for extra strength and to prevent the silver from tarnishing. Although platinum had been known as early as the 16th century in Colombia, it had not been extensively used in jewellery before the turn of the century because of the difficulties involved in working it, but from then on it became the favourite metal of the jeweller, and earrings set mainly in platinum were produced until the 1940s.

Around 1915 one can discern a change in the design of earrings from the garland type to a form that anticipates features of 1920s earrings. They tend to become longer and their typical form is that of an elongated baton-shaped motif usually set with diamonds, supporting a drop, often a pearl or a larger millegrain-set diamond. Of course the majority of these earrings continue to possess features typical of earlier periods: they are entirely white, set with diamonds and pearls, in accordance with the general preference for monochromatic and pale coloured jewels in vogue since the late 19th century, and furthermore they continue to display the characteristic delicate

p. 126

A pair of diamond pendent earrings in the garland style, circa 1900.

millegrain settings and fine foliate details. On the other hand the pronounced elongation and geometrical details foreshadow the designs of the following decade. They also well suited the female silhouette as recently redesigned by the Parisian couturier Paul Poiret, who liberated women from corsets with the introduction of fluid, high-waisted dresses. The emphasis in fashion was on straight, vertical lines which were counterbalanced by long sautoirs and long pendent earrings. An example of earrings p. 156 where old and new features coexist is a pair of French platinum and diamond pendent earrings. The overall design and the millegrain settings conform to the garland style, while the size and length of the drop, and the geometrical mitre-shaped surmount anticipate earrings of the 1920s. Another interesting example is the elaborate pair of p. 157 chandelier-design earrings, where the floral and foliate design is typical of the garland style but the size and tassel motifs are already Art Deco in spirit.

It was during these years that the screw fitting to clamp the earring to the lobe, which had first been developed in the last years of the 19th century, gained popularity. Its advantage over traditional types of fitting was that it avoided the necessity of piercing the lobe, a practice which had begun to be regarded as barbaric. This was symptomatic of the general move towards liberating women from traditional constraints, exemplified in the field of fashion by the rejection of harmful items of clothing such as tightly laced corsets, and in social and political life by the movement to establish votes for women.

Decade by decade: the 1920s
The outbreak of the First World War in 1914 brought a sudden end to the frivolous period of the Belle Epoque. Jewellery production ceased: precious metals and gemstones became scarce; platinum, an important material for the manufacture of nitric acid for explosives and for engine magnetos, disappeared from jewellery workshops; craftsmen turned their skills from jewellery to the armament industry, and women were forced to take up the jobs left vacant by men called to the front. By the end of the war in 1918, the newly emancipated women had adopted an androgynous look: they had shortened their dresses and cut their hair '*à la garconne*' thus dispensing for the first time in history with what St Paul called their 'crowning glory.' Consequently earrings, more than ever, came to play a role of paramount importance by filling the gap between the bob and the shoulders, echoing the simple vertical line of the dress while adding a touch of frivolity and femininity to the new masculine look. During the 1920s earrings undoubtedly became the most important form of jewellery, as can be seen in contemporary portraiture, photographs, advertisements, theatre and fashion designs, such as those by Jeanne Lanvin. Furthermore, the great number of surviving 1920s earrings indicates both their popularity and copious production.

The common characteristic of all earrings of the early and mid-1920s was their very pronounced vertical and geometrical line and the use of enamels and gemstones

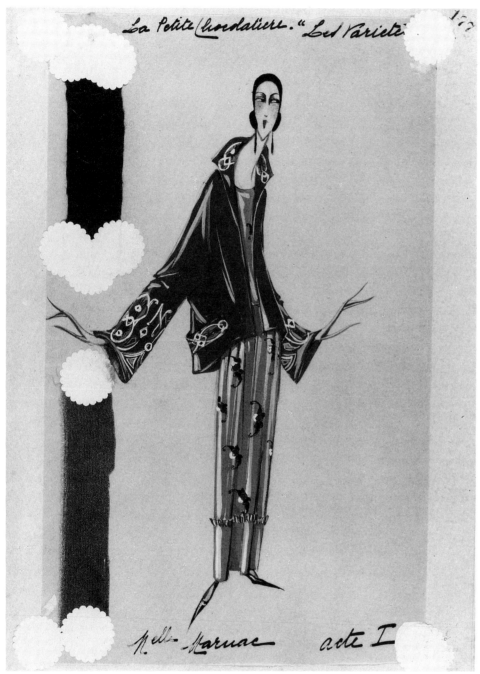

La Petite Chocolatiere. "Les Variété[...]

Mlle Marnac   acte I

Left: a pencil and gouache theatrical design by Jeanne Lanvin, October 1922. Note the long torpedo-shaped pendent earrings.

Below: a pencil and gouache fashion design by Jeanne Lanvin, March 1924. Note the elongated carved coral torped-shaped pendent earrings.

MIKADO.

of striking and contrasting colours. These daring new juxtapositions of colours were realized by the combination of precious gemstones such as emeralds, rubies, sapphires and diamonds with semiprecious stones such as onyx, coral, jade, rock crystal, turquoise and lapis lazuli, the latter frequently carved into cylinders, circles, oblong panels and drops. Good examples are the coral and onyx pendent earrings where the bright red coral drop carved in a floral design is suspended from a long chain of black onyx baton motifs. The interest in such vivid colours derived from Diaghilev's Ballets Russes which made such an impact on Paris and London society around 1910: their bright juxtapositions of colours both in the costumes and stage sets shocked and

p. 158

fascinated audiences and at the same time set the tone for the jewellery and fashion of the following decade.

Besides novel and striking combinations of colour, there were innovative features in the setting and cut of stones. The favourite new style of setting gems was the 'pavé', in which the gems paved the whole surface of the mount. This was often achieved by cutting the stones to fit the required shape of the mount and of the decorative pattern. It is clearly visible in the long pendent earrings designed by Boucheron, where emer- p. 155 alds, rubies and sapphires are cut with domed surfaces to fit into the stylized floral design on a diamond ground. It is interesting to note that besides the interest in contrasting colours emphasis was also placed on the difference between matt and polished surfaces, something that can be seen once again in the illustrated earrings by Boucheron; diamonds provide a sparkling surface while the coloured gemstones provide the matt.

It is not surprising that earrings such as these, possessing most of the novel features of the time (the pronounced elongated line, the stylized, almost geometrical, floral pattern and the juxtaposition of colour and texture) were selected for the Exposition International des Arts Décoratifs et Industrielles Modernes in 1925, an exhibition held in Paris with the purpose of presenting to the public novel and modern design. It is from the abbreviated title of the exhibition, 'Art Déco', that the popular name for the style of the mid-1920s and early 1930s derives.

Although jewellers working in this style found sources of inspiration in the artistic traditions of countries as exotic and far apart as Egypt and China, Persia and India or Japan, the most influential eastern tradition for earrings was that of China. Chinese jade plaques carved and pierced in traditional Chinese motifs of gourds, leaves and peonies, and symbolic Chinese 'BI' were imported directly from the East and mounted by famous western jewellers as long earring pendants. The great popularity p. 154 of this type of earring is demonstrated by its appearance in numerous variations in the pages of earring designs of the time by Cartier London. Green jade combined with stones such as onyx and diamonds suited the striking colour schemes of Art Deco – green, black and white – and offered an interesting combination of matt and polished surfaces. Besides exploiting Chinese-crafted materials, jewellers also frequently included in their earrings imitative Chinese motifs such as stylized pagodas and lanterns. The latter is clearly recognizable in the design of a pair of French emerald and diamond pendent earrings of the mid-1920s reproduced here. p. 159

Another feature typical of pendent earrings of this time is that they are always mounted in platinum and, unlike some earlier types of earrings, are provided with stud rather than screw fittings. These consist of a prong soldered at the back of the earring, which is inserted into the pierced earlobe and secured by a small, usually hexagonal, plate. It is released by a spring mechanism triggered by pressing a little metal tongue projecting from the edge of the plate. This new type of fitting was more secure, and was desirable for several reasons. Firstly, women now led a much more active and dynamic life, and precious earrings might be worn at night while dancing to the frenetic rhythms of the Charleston; secondly, they were very fragile: as has been mentioned, a great number of earrings were set with long thin plaques carved in semiprecious stones such as jade, which could crack if dropped; and thirdly, it was unobtrusive, a most important feature now that the back of the ear was visible with the newly cropped bob. All Cartier's examples seem to have been attached in this way.

In the late 1920s long pendent earrings continued in favour, but they can be distinguished from their earlier counterparts by their fuller, usually triangular or lozenge-shaped outline reminiscent of a chandelier, hence the name 'chandelier earrings'. This tendency is clearly visible in the magnificent pair of pearl and diamond earrings made by Cartier in London in 1928. Their shape is undoubtedly inspired by a crystal chandelier with central drop, stylized sconces and candles. A second development is the gradual submergence of colours, to be replaced by the whiteness of pearl and diamonds. Contrast was achieved by combining in the setting a variety of diamonds of different cuts: baguettes, marquise, trapeze, crescent-, triangular-, pear-shaped, and brilliant-cut diamond, all of which reflect light in different ways. Coloured gemstones did not entirely disappear; a beautiful example is the bell-shaped pair of earrings set with diamonds and Indian ruby beads, by Drayson of London. It is interesting to note how the choice of the gemstone influences the design of the earring, reminiscent of a bell-shaped Jaipur enamel ear pendant.

p. 153

p. 160, 161

Towards the end of the decade the decorative arts were inspired by motifs deriving from industry and mechanical instruments: stylized motifs of nuts and bolts set with diamonds appear in earrings. Versatility became appreciated and jewels were constructed to be worn in different ways: a pair of bracelets could be combined to form a fashionable bandeau or sautoir and earrings could be combined together on a brooch mount, as in the last example shown on p. 159.

The 1930s

The 1930s are characterized by a revolutionary innovation in the history of earrings: the clip fitting. From Antiquity to the beginning of the 20th century, the only way of wearing an earring was to insert it or its suspension hook in a hole pierced in the lobe. As we have already seen, in the early 20th century the practice of piercing ears came to be considered barbaric, and this prompted the use of the screw fitting as an alternative. But although this did avoid piercing the lobe, it was not adequate to support heavy earrings. The clip fitting of the 1930s finally allowed women to wear heavy earrings without piercing their ears, and moreover, by securely clasping the lobe, enabled the earring for the first time to expand upward to decorate the upper part of the ear. Rosettes, stylized flowerheads, shells, cornucopias, ribbons, spirals, comets, stylized wings and curled leaves decorating the upper lobe were among the favourite earclips. In many cases, the upward curl of the design following the natural line of the ear meant designing one earclip for the right ear and another for the left, so that

p. 164, 165

A pair of stained blue chalcedony, sapphire and diamond earclips, probably by Belperron, circa 1935, each designed as a foliate motif, from the collection of jewellery of the Duchess of Windsor.

they were not interchangeable. The advertisement for Boucheron in the magazine *Femina* of March 1934 underlines the elegance of the new compact diamond earrings; they were well suited to the hairstyles of the time, which could either be short or long but had the hair gathered at the top or back in a bun and brushed away from the ears in fluid waves.

The ever fashionable hoop earring was also adapted to the new fitting: an open circle securely clipped to the lobe, giving the impression of passing through a non-existent hole. These clips, continuing the late 1920s trend, were set with variously cut diamonds in white metal mounts: white monochromatic jewels were still all the rage, coloured precious and semiprecious stones being used only sparingly to pick out the design. They often came as a set with the most characteristic jewel of the 1930s, the double-clip brooch the design of which they repeated on a reduced scale.

Although compact earclips were most popular at the time, the fashion for pendent earrings never completely died out and sometimes these 1930s earclips were provided with a pendant, a tassel, a drop, or a cascade of ribbons which could be attached to the lower part of the clip to make it more suitable for formal occasions, thus continuing the use of 'versatile' jewellery.

For evening wear during this period, long pendent earrings, again set with multicoloured gemstones, were in favour, their voluminous shapes distinguishing them quite clearly from 1920s examples. They tend to expand along the horizontal axis and lose the typical vertical character of the previous decade. Different and unusual cuts for the stones continued to be exploited for coloured stones as well as for diamonds, a good example being the two pairs of pendent earrings by Cartier London, 1931–32, set with aquamarines. By the late 1930s established firms were already anticipating motifs and designs which were to gain importance in the following decade. This is well exemplified by the pair of citrine and diamond pendent earrings made in 1937 by Cartier London, which are long and voluminous in form, set in yellow gold with diamonds and citrines of various shades of russet and golden yellow, something which heralds the use in 1940s jewellery of attractive coloured gemstones of comparatively low intrinsic value – citrine, aquamarines, amethysts. p. 162, 163

The 1940s

By 1940 earclips were predominant everywhere. They had large gold surfaces, replacing those set with diamonds, and more sculptural shapes such as fluttering ribbon bows, bouquets of flowers and fan-shaped motifs in contrast to the geometrical lines of the 1930s. After forty years of the supremacy of platinum in jewellery, gold came back on a large scale, and it is interesting to look at major jewellers' archives, where the transition from platinum to gold coincides with the new decade. This is very clear in the records of Boucheron Paris, where earrings produced until August 1938 are mounted in platinum, but from then on always in yellow gold. The preference for gold in jewellery also had an economic reason: at the outbreak of the war p. 170, 171 platinum was again requisitioned by the armaments industry and the jeweller had to make the most of the scarce gold on the market. The regulations controlling the use of precious metals were extremely strict, especially in France. Anyone who wished to commission a piece of jewellery in gold had to supply the raw material of which twenty per cent would go to the state. Consequently jewellery was made of very thin gold, frequently of low carat. At the same time, the irregular supply of precious gemstones, such as diamonds from South Africa and rubies and sapphires from Burma and Siam, caused a scarcity on the market. This prompted the resetting of gemstones mounted in older pieces of jewellery and the widespread use of synthetic rubies and sapphires. When precious stones were used they were either small and inexpensive or (in the case of sapphires and rubies) synthetic. Semiprecious gemstones were favoured – topaz, aquamarine, amethyst and citrine being relatively cheap yet often large in size and highly effective. In spite of the great difficulties in the turmoil of war, jewellery remained a valuable source of portable capital, and therefore went on being designed, produced and sold. The angular geometrical designs of the late 1930s were not entirely discontinued. This may be seen in mitre-shaped earclips, where the accentuated geometrical design corresponds with 1930 earclips, but the choice of stones, usually citrines and small rubies, heralds the new style. As in all periods of transition one finds old and new elements merging together.

The change is clearly visible if one looks at a page of Boucheron's archival records. Among the designs registered for 1938 one finds earclips characterized by rigid and geometric forms (such as no. 11.306 and no. 35.354216) and a severe linear inverted U-shaped earclip, set with calibré-cut rubies. From 1940 onwards all the designs are naturalistic, and the success and popularity of the curled leaf earclip in polished gold is attested by its consecutive orders. According to the records this model was repeated and sold 14 times from December 1941 to September 1945. Another motif was an attractive gem-set flower spray held together by fluttering ribbon ties. All the naturalistic earclips are fairly compact in form, filling the lobe or following the contour of the ear. Characteristically they continue to present rather stiff features lacking movement and fluidity: the ribbon ties knotted in bows are always realized in wide surfaces of polished gold which contribute to a bold and static impression. Other favoured motifs displaying similar characteristics are rosettes and plain ribbon bows such as in the design by Mauboussin, rosette and ribbons combined together, and scrolled drape motifs. A particularly striking example of the latter type was produced by Hoeffer & Trabert, the American branch of Mauboussin; they are typically asymmetrical and rigid in design with a scrolled surface of polished white gold and a large step-cut aquamarine at the centre, the border set with small rubies and diamonds. They are accompanied by a large brooch of identical design set with an extremely large central aquamarine, which reflects an American preference for large and flamboyant jewels. The set of earclips and matching brooch or clip is a typical feature of this period. Such heavy brooches, worn on the lapel of tailored

p. 171

p. 167

p. 166

suits, had completely supplanted the double clip brooch which had been so popular in the 1930s.

Though compact earclips were the favourite type of ear ornament, pendent earrings were not completely dismissed. The extant examples and records in archives indicate that the pendent element is often very flimsy compared to the bold surmount often consisting of two chains with various terminations such as a cone or gold beads. One sees this, for instance, in earclip with a gold scrolled surmount supporting fine p. 168 chain drops, which have to be regarded more as minor decorative elements than as pendants in their own right since they are not at all in proportion with the volume of the surmount. Again this is visible in earrings by Mellerio, both those made in 1946, set with a large topaz held by two chains tied in a knot which hang down as pendants, and those of stylized cornucopia design of 1947 which suspend five bead chains. Further evidence may be found in Boucheron's archive designs of 1943, where tubular chains of articulated links form the pendent element of entwined ribbon surmounts. Besides earrings, necklaces and bracelets were often decorated with chain tassels similar to those found on pendent earrings. A few earrings with more voluminous pendants were also created, such as those formed of two chains of gold graduated disc motifs by Boucheron, or the 'Ferronière' earrings of 1944 by Mellerio, designed as a graduated line of curled gold wire. Although attractive, these long earrings did not gain the same popularity as the compact earclips.

In the mid-1940s there was a vogue for light-hearted earrings, amusing and friv- p. 190 olous designs like the small pendent watches with the dial in a border of calibre-cut sapphires designed by Van Cleef & Arpels, or miniature buckle and belt motifs commonly known as *jarretières*.

As the 1940s decade was coming to its close, earclips began to show greater movement and lightness, with gold surfaces being broken up in woven patterns or worked into twisted rope motifs combined with coloured gemstones such as turquoises and amethysts; naturalistic patterns of flowers characterized by a greater sense of movement began to prevail over scrolled drape motifs, heralding the design of the new decade, the 1950s.

Four designs from a catalogue by Van Cleef & Arpels, made between 1945 and 1950.

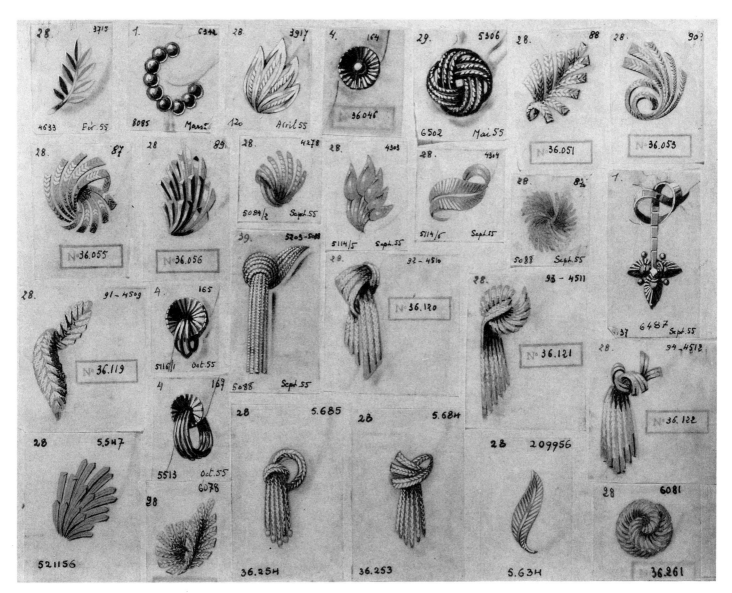

The 1950s

The hairstyles of the 1950s gave women complete freedom to wear their hair piled on the top of the head, knotted on the nape in a tight chignon or in short or medium-length coiffures brushed away from the ears; all these styles were appropriate for displaying both long pendent earrings and compact clips. After a decade in which large surfaces of yellow or red gold and clips of bold, stiff and sculptural design had reigned supreme, long pendent earrings set with opulent rainfalls of diamonds in white metal mounts returned triumphantly.

The economic boom which followed the deprived war years, coupled with the desire to celebrate a return to a more relaxed and uninhibited life-style, led to the

Part of a page of earring design of the 1950s from Boucheron Archives, showing the variety of shapes fashionable at the time.

development of an aesthetic in design which aimed at free, light and functional lines. Jewellery abandoned the straight, angular lines of Art Deco, and the large bulky forms of the 1940s, and evolved new, light, curvy, aerodynamic shapes which conveyed a sense of movement. The sources of inspiration were extremely varied, as were the ways they were interpreted; naturalism, abstraction, exoticism and conventionalism happily coexisted to suit the different tastes of women, who were free to choose whatever style they preferred after the many years of uniformity of fashion during the war.

The feminine 'new look' launched by Dior in 1947 remained, with slight variations, in fashion for a decade, and the exuberant lines of his evening gowns characterized by narrow waists, frothy and puffy ample skirts, and above all the generous décolleté and pointed, heart-shaped necklines, prompted the production of a vast selection of pendent earrings of curvy, free and informal line. Diamonds were, without any doubt, the gemstone *par excellence* for these important creations and maintained their supremacy throughout the 1950s. They suited the rich brocades, embroidered silks and precious laces of evening dresses, and were an ideal companion to the mink coat, then at the height of its popularity, by adding a touch of glitter to the face surrounded by the dark gleam of a fur collar.

The great variety of forms included all sorts of curved and fluid shaped surmounts, supporting long and voluminous articulated tassels or cascades of similarly cut diamonds. The design of the surmount was extremely varied, sometimes reviving the clip of 1930s inspiration, sometimes opting for a more naturalistic form, and sometimes choosing abstract shapes inspired by contemporary experiments in the visual arts. Rosettes, entwined ribbons, curved leaves, flowerheads, scrolls and question marks, turbans, shooting stars and fans are just a few of the motifs for surmounts, while below would hang articulated drops reminiscent of waterfalls, cascades of leaves, festoons, waterdrops, tassels and clusters of flowers. Glittering earrings drew attention to eyes made languid and feminine by heavy lines of eyeliner pointing up at the sides. A magnificent example is that designed by Van Cleef & Arpels with a 1930s inspired rosette surmount above a rich and fluid cascade of baguette and pear-shaped diamond drops. Pearls were as much a favourite as diamonds, and earrings designed as a scrolled surmount with a pearl drop or a pearl suspended from a chain of baguette diamonds were produced in many variations. Although overshadowed by the popularity of diamonds, coloured stones such as emeralds, rubies and sapphires often added a touch of colour to otherwise monochromatic evening creations.

The metal used for these important creations *de grande soir* was invariably white. Platinum returned, white gold was widely used, and palladium, the lightest metal of the platinum group, made its appearance: lightness of the mount was an essential factor in the creation of these long and voluminous pendent earrings which otherwise would have been uncomfortable to wear. A further demonstration of this preference

p. 172, 173

p. 175

for lightness is the practice, in the early 1950s, of channel-setting small baguette diamonds in rail-like mounts, while towards the end of the decade the stones were held in place by minute claws. It was a pride of the great jewellers to create mounts where the metal was so reduced that it was practically invisible.

Although pendent earrings were the most fashionable form of ear ornament for evening wear, compact earclips were also popular, and many of the examples described above were designed so that the long drop (up to 6 or 8cms) could be detached and the surmount worn by itself. Other diamond-set short earrings assumed the shape of turbans, helixes or flowerhead clusters. A favourite design, simple yet very successful, consisted of a single pearl or mabe pearl surrounded by a foliate border of variously cut diamonds, while more elaborate examples assumed the shapes of exotic diamond flowers such as fuchsias and orchids, with a short pearl drop. A particularly p. 174 successful model was designed by Van Cleef & Arpels in the late 1940s as a stylized fuchsia with diamond petals and short pearl drop: it gained great favour in the 1950s and its popularity continues today with slight alteration. The same may be said of the diamond-set turban supporting an acorn drop mounted with pearls often of different p. 175 colours, designed by Verdura in 1953.

The great majority of these earrings, both long and short, were provided with a clip or, less frequently, with a screw fitting. Pierced ears were definitely out of fashion in the fifties, probably not because they were thought to be wrong in any way, as in the early part of the century, but because of the unsightly effect of a pierced earlobe when earrings were not worn. Indeed they came to be considered socially improper for the well-to-do lady and confined to the lower classes. Women who had already had their ears pierced concealed the holes with clip on earrings.

Four designs in pencil and gouache by Boucheron, March–September 1955. The first has a rosette surmount suspended with a cascade of bagouette and brilliant-cut diamonds, the second is designed as a stylized leaf supporting a cascade of baguette diamonds; the third and fourth are also cascades set with baguette and brilliant-cut diamonds, the last supporting a larger brilliant-cut diamond drop.

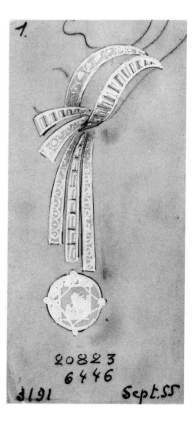

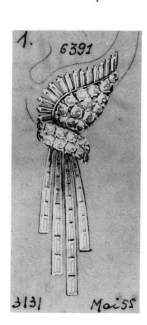

Yellow gold was the favourite material for daywear earrings which were usually p. 139, 174, 175 short, in the shape of rosettes, fans, hoops of Creole inspiration, leaves of stylized or naturalist form, spirals, turbans, florets, helixes and clusters, at times decorated with drops and tassels. The ribbons and bows of the 1940s continued in lighter and often informally sketched forms, often combined with leaves and sprays of flowers. Typical of these earrings of the 1950s was the varied and imaginative use of the metal, worked into corded wires, pleats, passementeries, woven or fretted patterns and tubular or plated chains sparingly set with small diamonds or coloured stones such as turquoises, sapphires, rubies and emeralds, combined in interesting chromatic contrasts, as seen in the examples designed by Mellerio and Van Cleef & Arpels.

Among the most typical earclips of the time is that designed as a 'boule' of gold wire, set with different combinations of gemstones such as rubies and turquoises (the favourite semiprecious stone of the fifties), or rubies and sapphires with diamonds.

First created by Cartier in 1952, the design was immediately copied and reinterpreted in many variations by most of the jewellers of the time.

Contemporary daywear fashions were dominated by the classic two-piece suit reintroduced by Chanel at the reopening of her atelier in 1954, and these yellow gold earrings suited them perfectly, as well as the stylish afternoon dresses then in vogue.

Earrings simply mounted with a single pearl, natural or cultured, often of large size without any form of decorative surmount, gained in popularity throughout the decade thanks to their adaptability to both day and evening dresses and to their discreet sheen which always flattered the features of the face without being as overpowering as diamonds. Cultured pearls came back into favour after a decade of neglect; and natural pearls, whose price had dropped dramatically in the 1920s when cultured pearls became widely available, were admired again and rose in value. As cheaper alternatives, large mabe pearls were favoured within gold and diamond borders.

Left and opposite: three pencil designs for gold and gem-set earrings, by Mellerio, 1950s.

143

A pair of 18ct molten gold, diamond and baroque pearl earclips by Andrew Grima, 1968. The stylized flowerhead surmounts support detachable pendants.

The 1960s

In the 1960s the marked distinction between very precious earrings set with diamonds for the evening and less expensive gold earrings for the day disappears. All types could be worn at all times provided that they were large and decorative. Their effect was achieved not necessarily by using materials of high intrinsic value, but by exploiting contrasts of texture and colour. A good example of this style is a pair of opal, emerald, sapphire and diamond pendent earrings mounted in yellow gold in 1966 by Andrew Grima, a particularly successful jeweller and designer who can be regarded as the trendsetter of the sixties style in Britain. His earrings are typical of the time in their abstract design and in their interplay of different textures, the rough gold mounts contrasting with the smooth and polished surface of the opals. Their vivid use of colour is also typical; the bright green emeralds, the intense blue sapphires and the bright multicoloured flashes of opals highlighted with diamonds and gold are particularly striking. It is not surprising that these eyecatching earrings won the 1966 Duke of Edinburgh Prize for Elegant Design, the first and only time that a piece of hand-made jewellery rather than an industrial product gained this prestigious award. The judges' report stated that British jewellery designers 'are now starting to win an international reputation for their imaginative work . . . There is a much less inhibited attitude to new techniques, such as melting under controlled temperatures and new ways of giving different textures to gold. These have given much greater scope to the designer and have released him from the rigid conventions of setting – and much credit for this liberation, and for the gaiety that has resulted, must go to Andrew Grima, the recipient of the 1966 prize.'

p. 179

Similar qualities are to be found in Italian clips set with emeralds, sapphires and gold. The amoeba-like abstraction of their design once again combines contrasting elements: the large cabochon emerald with its smooth and polished surface in contrast with the textured gold mount, and the striking use of colour: green, blue and yellow. The emeralds and sapphires, although not of gem quality, have been exploited for their attractive colour, once again indicating how contemporary jewellers were often more interested in the decorative quality of the gemstones than in their intrinsic value.

p. 177

The use of uncut gemstones and natural objects unworked by man was widespread at the time, and jewellers in most countries were eager to exploit such materials. Emphasis was placed on the contrast between faceted and uncut stones, such as agate geodes, aggregates of amethyst or dioptase crystals left in their natural form. In one pair of long pendent earrings, sapphires, diamonds and fragments of crystal dioptase are combined with rough-textured gold-work reminiscent of entwined branches. Interest in unusual textures, striking colour combinations and relatively cheap materials prompted jewellers such as David Webb and Verdura in New York and Darde et Fils in Paris to make use of exotic and colourful sea shells for their earrings. The bold contours of the *polymita picta* (Cuban tree snails) with brown, orange, yellow and white stripes applied with gold lozenges by David Webb (1964–65) or with gold saw-teeth by Darde et Fils show how such materials can be successfully used. All the examples reproduced here belonged to the Duchess of Windsor, who like other fashionable women of the mid-sixties did not disdain comparatively inexpensive earclips provided that they were unusual and decorative. All sorts of shells of differing shapes were adopted to both short and long earrings, as is illustrated by the extraordinary late sixties example by Grima, where an elongated tusk-shaped shell from the South Pacific is enclosed in a gold wire case and its natural curve exploited to echo the contour of the face.

Nature, transmuted in abstract and stylized forms, was the source of inspiration for many ear ornaments: for example, the intricate form of sprawling roots is the basis for gold mounts in the earclips designed by the American jeweller Arthur King, where the central cultured pearl or smooth coral bead is held in a surround of textured and entwined gold wire-work. In a similar way small gold batons soldered together, framing the large sapphires in Grima's 1968 earclips, are reminiscent of the twigs in birds' nests, while in a pair of decorative and exuberant earrings by Meister of Zurich (designed in 1971 but very much in the style of the 1960s) clusters of mimosa blossom are juxtaposed with polished gold spheres and brilliant-cut diamonds. Abstract forms and different textures, consistent features of 1960s jewels and earrings, were achieved by means of new techniques such as melting under controlled temperatures. The results can be seen in the gold and coral earclips by Sterlé where the gold mount appears as 'frozen' molten metal, or in the jagged textured gold edges of Marit Aschan's earclips of 1966, reminiscent of butterflies dipped into turquoise enamel encrusted with diamonds. One of those who has continued since the 1960s to achieve infinite variations of texture in gold is Gerda Flockinger. In a stunning combination of interchangeable earrings of 1980, the inherent beauty of the molten gold is emphasized by minute grains and swirled encrustations where tiny diamonds sparkle at random. Most of these innovative examples are one-off productions and reflect the greater importance attached to creative design rather than intrinsic value; in fact, the jewels in their settings are worth considerably more than their break-up value, which indicates both that people are buying more for beauty of design than for investment

p. 177, 178

p. 189

A pair of gold, enamel and diamond star-shaped earclips with matching brooch, and a pair of gold, ruby and diamond earclips designed as flowerhead clusters, both by Boucheron, Paris, circa 1970.

p. 178, 179

and that the designer is achieving a personal status very different from the anonymity of his immediate predecessors. Examples produced in larger quantities and not as one-offs were manufactured for a more conventional clientele, and although not as daring as the designs by Grima, Sterlé or Marit Aschan they display characteristic sixties elements. This is noticeable in the pair of stylized flowerhead earclips by Kutchinsky, where the theme, naturalistic this time and not abstract, is made vivid by bright and smooth green and blue enamel juxtaposed with the rough textured gold border.

Other fashionable earrings, especially for day wear, were inspired by objects, plants and animals that had not been associated with jewellery in previous decades. Some of them are distinctly light-hearted, such as the frog earclips in gold and bright green enamel with cabochon ruby eyes which David Webb presented to the Duchess of Windsor in 1964; or the pineapple earclips set with stripes of calibré-cut onyx and rubies designed in 1968 by Jean Schlumberger. Surrealist themes in jewellery had already been pioneered in the mid-fifties by artists such as Salvador Dali; the 'Honey-comb Heart' earclips of 1954 studded with circular-cut rubies and diamonds, and paired gold wing earclips signed 'Dali' in black enamel are good examples. But it is only in the sixties that one witnesses in jewellery a proliferation of such witty and amusing motifs. They represented a break with tradition and went hand-in-hand with the vogue for all that was fun, innovative and daring and they suited the fashion that replaced Dior's sophisticated New Look and opulent but measured elegance with 'alternative' clothes – trousers and miniskirts – and required 'alternative' jewels to match. This new social and moral climate of the sixties found expression in such outward signs as the geometric and sculpted dress of Courrèges or Paco Rabanne, the miniskirt of Mary Quant, the severe and short bob devised by Vidal Sassoon – and amusing unconventional earrings.

At the same time traditional examples of high intrinsic value continued to be produced. These were designed as diamond-set stylized flowerhead clusters supporting opulent cascades, but their jagged contours, achieved by alternating brilliant-cut and marquise-shaped diamonds held in minute white precious metal claws, differentiate them from the flowing and continuous lines set mainly with baguette diamonds of the previous decade.

The 1970s

After 1970 earring design, like fashions in dress and hairstyle, seems to break free from all constraint and to become almost infinitely varied. The only common feature is largeness.

One of the most characteristic types of earring for day wear was a pendant designed as a large circular, oval or drop-shaped hoop held by a smaller surmount of similar design. These were mainly carved in hardstones including rock crystal, lapis lazuli, onyx, coral, tortoiseshell and ivory or rare woods like *bois d'armourette*, or they could be made of gold, often decorated with bright contrasting enamels such as blue with yellow and red. The popularity of this hoop pattern was such that one finds it is p. 184, 185 repeated both in designs and extant examples from all the major jewellery firms. Van Cleef & Arpels and Mauboussin were famous for their pear-shaped onyx hoops embellished with gold and diamond motifs suspended on variously shaped surmounts, such as the example illustrated on p. 184, where the elongated onyx hoop decorated with pavé-set diamond motifs hangs from a leaf-shaped surmount of brilliant-cut diamonds. Often these earrings came with a long chain necklace – the most typical jewel of the seventies – formed of similarly designed links suspending a large pendant which repeated, in an enlarged form, the motif of the earring. Boucheron favoured an upside-down drop-shaped surmount with a similarly designed but larger drop in gold, lapis lazuli, tiger's eye, or pink coral (e.g., model nos: 37640, 37632, 37631 and 37750 of 1970 and 1971). The great popularity of the pendent hoop earring was also exploited by Mellerio, who did not limit himself to two hoops but designed examples with three, made of textured or corded gold linked together. Besides the repetition of the pendent hoop motif, another noticeable feature of most jewellers and above all of Boucheron's production is the use of vivid and striking colour combinations, such as pink-green-gold, brown-pink, brown-green, turquoise-purple, light blue-black-gold and red-black-white. Hoop earrings were all made of gold or carved in hardstone; they were frequently decorated with pavé-set diamond motifs but never with faceted coloured gemstones.

Hoop earrings were also widespread in the USA; David Webb in New York became celebrated for his large rock crystal and diamond drop earrings with pear-shaped hoops carved in rock crystal and embellished with diamonds. The design was devised one day when he happened to see a crystal chandelier being dismantled. His heart sank at the sight of such wonderful drops being wasted and he thought immediately of earrings. His design was so successful that these earrings continued to be produced well into the 1980s.

During the 1970s the most important jewellery houses such as Boucheron, Cartier, and Van Cleef & Arpels were differentiating between unique creations set with exceptional gemstones made on commission and more readily available products at more affordable prices intended for a wider but still discriminating clientèle. Many of the examples mentioned above were included in the 'boutique' line of these jewellers and were meant for the fashion-conscious woman who was free to chose her own jewels according to taste and the colours of her clothes. The idea was to own several pairs of earrings of different colours which would be changed to suit various occasions.

The great popularity of the hoop-in-hoop motif meant that it was also adopted for evening wear. When that happened, a more precious version was produced, either set entirely with diamonds (as the earrings by Gérard 1978–79, where the three p. 184 hoops suspended from a cluster surmount are claw-set throughout with brilliant-cut diamonds) or with the hoops enlivened by coloured precious stones such as rubies, emeralds and sapphires alternately set with diamonds (as can be seen in some designs by Boucheron, nos: 37731 and 120971). Other precious examples for the evening p. 185 repeated a similar outline of the hoop pendants but the hollow centre was filled with encrustations of exotic decorative motifs set with differently coloured gemstones. The inspiration of many of these earrings was Indian; the red and green colours, as in the Boucheron example of 1978, suggest the combination of colours in Jaipur enamels; and the use of cabochon stones in flowerhead arrangements of gemstones is typical of Indian 18th- and 19th-century traditional jewellery. This source of inspiration is confirmed by some of the names given to designs of this period such as: Arabesque, Sultan, Nepal. It is not surprising that the Middle East and India inspired earring design, for many aspects of artistic, cultural and intellectual life in the 1970s were influenced by the East.

The short earring was often designed as a half-hoop or a hoop simply clamped to the earlobe with a clip fitting. Like pendants, they were made either of yellow gold, variously textured and worked, or set with coloured semiprecious hardstones embellished with diamonds. It is interesting to note that throughout the seventies the metal used for setting all gemstones including diamonds was yellow gold and not platinum or white gold; since the 18th century diamonds had almost invariably been set in white metal to increase the whiteness of the stones, and only in the 1970s did the jewellers switch to yellow gold. This probably has several explanations: firstly the influence of traditional Indian jewels where diamonds were set in gold; secondly a desire to break with tradition; and thirdly an attempt to make diamond, the gemstone *par excellence*, more wearable at any time of the day and give a more casual look to the most glamorous and evening-orientated gem; the warmth of the metal and its association with daytime jewellery made such adornments more wearable. Obviously there were disadvantages in using gold with diamonds, for example high colour, very white stones appearing of lower quality when reflecting the yellow gold mount. On the other hand diamonds known as Cape stones which possess a yellow tint look better in a yellow gold than in a white gold or platinum setting. The seventies fashion for large earrings, cabochon coloured gemstones and above all the use of gold as the sole metal for setting all gemstones, and especially diamonds, are features which continued to be popular in the following decade.

The 1980s

In the 1980s earrings became so fashionable that they might be considered the jewel of the decade. Leading jewellers in Europe and the United States agree that by far the best selling jewels of the period were earrings. They were the favourite of the fashion-conscious woman, often being worn as the sole form of jewelled ornament. They were considered an indispensable fashion accessory to match and complement the style of an outfit, whether that of the executive woman in a tailored Armani suit by day or the extravagant and feminine woman in a Lacroix gown by night. This explains why women of the eighties owned numerous pairs of earrings and never felt that they had enough. Furthermore, earrings, unlike rings, have no sentimental implications, and can be bought, given as a gift or changed without a second thought. Demand stimulated supply – from mass-produced types marketed in large numbers to the most exclusive and one-off creations. But they all, short or long, followed a certain

p. 180, 181 pattern: they had to be bold, flashy, large and colourful. Designs in this period are extremely eclectic, but all short earrings are characterized by large, bold yet compact shapes, while pendant earrings may be distinguished by their large sculptural and three-dimensional drops which differ from the elongated linear hoops of the previous decade.

Among day earrings there was another archaeological revival, largely promoted by Bulgari who since the mid-seventies had been mounting earrings with ancient p. 186 coins. Greek, Roman and even 17th- and 18th-century coins, known as '*gemme nummarie*', numismatic gems, were set in sleek mounts of matt or shiny metals of differing colours. Striking effects were obtained by juxtaposing ancient, worn materials with smooth and sleek modern mounts and by combining metals of contrasting colours. An example is the combination of gold and silver in the 1982 gold earclips set with a silver *drachm* of Demetrios I Soter, Syria (162–150 BC); platinum, gold and electrum are placed next to one another in the 1984 clips set with two electrum *hecte* struck in the island of Lesbos at Mytilene between 440 and 350 BC, held within concentric platinum and gold circles; and bronze or steel in combination with more precious materials became a distinctive feature of Bulgari and was employed in bold and innovative creations. Modernity is opposed to antiquity in the hoop earclips of p. 186 1980 designed as a graduated white gold band of flattened tubular linking set at the centre with two *fanam* yellow gold coins of the Dutch Indies (1719–40). Although coins might seem rather uninteresting and repetitive to the layman, the variety of these earclips is astonishing: coins appear singly or in pairs, and the mounts display an unlimited variety of decorative patterns: reeded or corded wires, concentric sections, fluted elements and flattened tubular chains sometimes embellished with a few diamonds or cabochon coloured gemstones and small pearls. A compact circular form is common, since it is demanded by the shape of the coin, and a genuine archaeological concern has led to the mounts always being inscribed with the provenance and denomination of the coins.

Archaeologically inspired earrings were not limited to Italy: the Greek jeweller p. 187 Ilias Lalaounis had been designing such jewels since the late 1950s but his earrings gained popularity in the eighties, with their large size and decorative bold shapes. His designs have since been copied and reinterpreted by many other jewellers in Greece and throughout Europe.

Lalaounis' earrings are inspired by the work of ancient Greek and Byzantine goldsmiths. Sometimes they are outstanding for their closeness to original ancient examples, while at others they are pastiches of Classical and Hellenistic themes, such as lions' or rams' heads, reminiscent of Greek late Classical earrings. All are in matt 18-carat gold, attempting to match the colour and texture of ancient examples. Reminiscent of Byzantine jewels are domed discs with granulation motifs encrusted with deep green emeralds and red rubies combined with pearls.

The fact that women want to own many pairs of earrings to suit different occasions has prompted the creation of large numbers made of relatively cheap materials which are nevertheless very attractive and eyecatching. Marina B in the 1980s had mastered this art by setting her highly innovative and decorative earrings with semiprecious stones of various colours combined with small diamonds, yellow gold, black burnished gold and black metal. In all this variety of materials and shapes (hearts, tassels, drops, hoops) the unifying element is the striking way in which colours are combined with the sculptural, three-dimensional form of both the surmounts and the drops. For example the *Cimin* model of 1987 inspired by a Chinese lantern is in bur- p. 181 nished black gold set with six blue topazes, yellow citrines, and amethysts, two pink tourmalines and diamonds. Among the most successful creations of Marina B is the *Pneus* earring, first designed in 1980, characterized by a squat circular pendant p. 183 inspired by the pneumatic tyre of an aeroplane – hence the name. In this type the circular drop, carved in semiprecious gemstones, can be changed for similar drops of differently coloured stones such as pink tourmaline, rock crystal or blue topaz in order to match the colour schemes of different outfits.

p. 183

Pendent earrings with wide and voluminous drops and compact clips in the form of large discs or fat crescents in many variations remained in favour throughout the decade both in Europe and in the United States. Bulgari's output is still dominated by large earclips such as those set with a pink sapphire flowerhead with emerald leaves at the centre of a cushion-shaped panel decorated with baguette and brilliant-cut diamonds; other motifs include open hearts set with sugar-loaf cabochons of precious stones of various cuts such as emeralds, rubies, sapphires and diamonds. A common characteristic of these colourful earrings is the imaginative and varied cuts of the gemstones which are shaped in order to fit the design: e.g., the tassel or baton-shaped

p. 181

quartzes of the 1984 Najwa earring by Marina B.

The typical fitting of these earrings is a combination of clip and stud. From the late seventies ear-piercing regained popularity, losing its negative connotations, mainly because earrings fixed through the lobe are much more secure. Safety and comfort are priorities when earrings are heavy. Some eighties earrings weigh up to 40 grams, and the weight, especially in large pendent earrings, is alleviated both by the spread of the surmount and by the additional clip fitting which enables it to be distributed over a larger surface. The combined clip-stud fitting also had the great advantage of being easily adaptable to the unpierced ear by sawing off the prong of the stud.

p. 182

As 'flash' is the essence of earrings of the eighties, in examples where coloured gemstones were not used, large surfaces of polished or hammered gold with diamonds were favoured, such as the large disc-shaped earclips retailed by Harry Winston, the bold crescents of the *Ecumes* by Marina B and the double twisted hoops by Repossi, all mounted in yellow gold pavé- or collet-set with diamonds. The glamour

p. 180, 189

of gold, its richness of colour and its reflective quality were exploited also by Paloma Picasso and Elsa Peretti. Both designing for Tiffany, they created earrings of very simple but bold shapes cast in gold. The glamorous effect of their stylized leaf, bean, cross, dome and hoop earrings is achieved by curving the polished gold surface and allowing it to reflect light in different ways. These earrings suited the taste of the emancipated woman of the eighties by combining feminine allure with the masculine look, gold and diamonds with cotton T-shirts and jeans.

The past decade has also witnessed an increase in the production of most lavish and expensive earrings set with exceptionally rare stones. In these cases the shapes tend to be fairly traditional, with the emphasis on the size and shape of the gemstone rather than the design.

The name of Harry Winston in New York has been traditionally associated with this lavish production. Among his most successful works are informal diamond cluster earclips, set with marquise and pear-shaped stones. The design was first created in the sixties but it has continued to be favoured until the present day, becoming a trade

p. 191

mark of the firm. A pair of the most recent cluster earclips by Harry Winston, made in 1989, is set with a total of 26 stones weighing 51.22 carats, remarkable not only for the weight but the quality of the stones which are all D (i.e., pure white) flawless.

This example may be distinguished from earlier clusters by its richer and more compact contour.

Cluster earclips are also used as surmounts to suspend detachable drops set with large gemstones such as emeralds, sapphires or diamonds. An exceptional example is the Harry Winston cluster tops with D flawless pear-shaped drops weighing 34.80 and 37.12 carats respectively. Large pear-shaped ruby earrings are never found because gem quality rubies are extremely rare and can hardly be matched. Lavish ruby earrings are always set with clusters of smaller stones, such as those set in hoop earrings by David Webb. p. 190, 191

The increasing quest for the perfect stone has meant that most high-quality gemstones set in important earrings are now accompanied by certificates from internationally recognized gemmological laboratories. The origin of coloured gemstones is stated; Columbia is prized for emeralds and Kashmir for sapphires; diamond certificates state the colour of the stone, with pure white (D) being the most sought after, and clarity is defined as the absence of internal impurities visible under ten-fold magnification. In recent years there has been growing interest in naturally coloured diamonds, blue, pink and yellow, and once again Harry Winston has been in the forefront. An example of 'fancy' coloured diamonds are those set with a yellow emerald-cut diamond in a border of six pear-shaped stones.

As the object of these earrings is to show off the stones, the mounts have a purely functional role with minimal impact of their own. This explains why the stones are held by minute claws which, in the case of high colour diamonds, are always in white metal. The result differs from the style of contemporary decorative earrings, where larger stones are nearly always collet-set in gold.

The rarity and value of these earrings derives both from the quality of the gemstones and the difficulty of matching them in perfect pairs, especially when one considers how many tons of diamond ore have to be sifted to find just 1 carat of gem quality diamond. p. 192

In the 1990s earrings show no sign of falling in popularity. Indeed their variety, splendour and ingenuity of design seem likely to rival any decade of the past. Costume jewellery, the demi-monde of the fashion world, has attained respectability and examples of it are often almost as expensive as the precious items they imitate or parody. The outrageous has become the commonplace, making it increasingly difficult to distinguish high from high-street fashion. An art form that has been flourishing for at least four thousand years is as alive as it ever was, as exciting, as beautiful and as unpredictable.

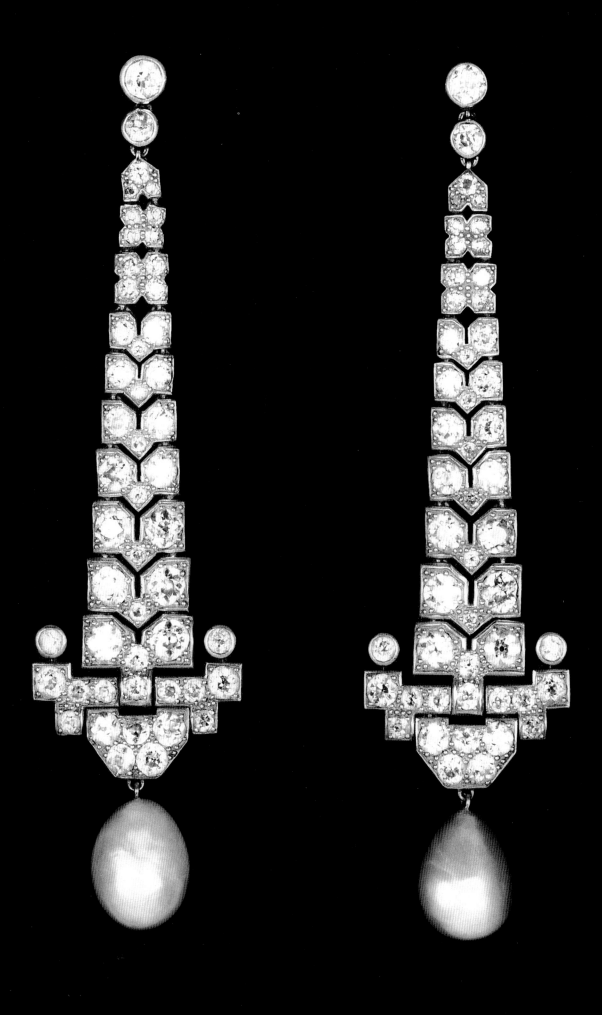

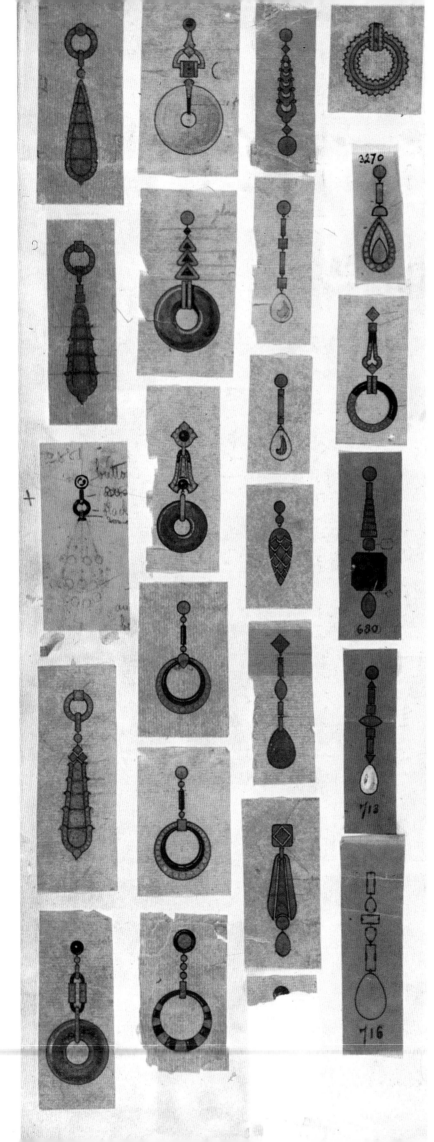

THE FASHIONABLE TWENTIES

Left: A collection of drawings from the archives of Cartier, London, depicting some of the most fashionable earring types of the years between 1923 and 1929. Particularly interesting are those suspended with jade and onyx hoops of different size. Common to all these earrings is the marked elongated vertical design. They are all set in platinum, mainly with pierced ear fittings; colour juxtapositions, such as the green of jade and the black of onyx, are vivid and often striking. The second example from the top in the second column (6 cms long) is set with a jade 'Bi' on a chain of triangular-cut onyx cabochons and brilliant-cut diamonds.

Above: A pair of carved jade, onyx and diamond pendent earrings, circa 1925. The chromatic contrast between apple green jade, white diamonds and shiny black onyx and enamel is typical of much Art Deco jewellery as is the use of carved jade directly imported from China. Note the fringe motifs which echo the trimmings of contemporary dresses.

Right: A Van Cleef & Arpels advertisement of the 1920s. The model wears a long string of pearls and very long pendent earrings set with diamonds and coloured gemstones emphatically geometrical in design.

Far right: A design for a pendent earring and a contemporary photograph of the final creation by Boucheron, exhibited at the Exposition des Arts Décoratifs of 1925 in Paris. It is representative of its time for the elongated shape and the stylized floral motifs set with domed *calibré*-cut coloured gemstones — emeralds, rubies, sapphires — on a ground of brilliant-cut diamonds.

Les Bijoux de Van Cleef & Arpels font le Tour du Monde pour parer la femme

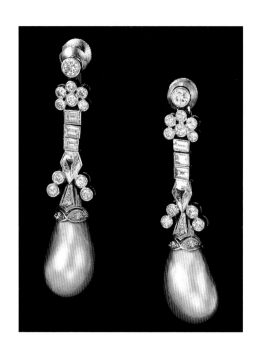

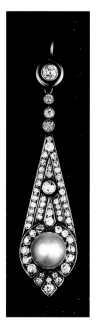

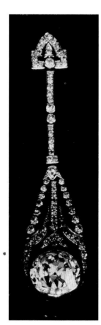

HARBINGERS OF ART DECO:
1915–1920

A collection of pendent earrings of the period 1915–20; their typical features are the delicate design and the platinum millegrain setting, which are still reminiscent of the delicacy of the garland style, and the elongated shape and geometrical motifs, which anticipate the style of earrings of the following decade. In line with the contemporary trend for black and white jewellery they are set mainly with diamonds and pearls, at times grey or black, as in, for example, the French pair of earrings set with silver-grey baroque pearls suspended from diamond chains of interlaced ribbon design (*above, upper right*). The pair of

attractive diamond pendent earrings of French manufacture visibly combine the millegrain setting of the garland style and elements typical of the 1920s such as the size and length of the drop and the mitre-shaped geometrical surmount (*above, lower right*). Again these features are visible in the elaborate diamond-set chandelier earrings, where floral and foliate motifs of the garland style are restrained within geometrical patterns and their size and fringed drops are already Art Deco in spirit (*opposite far right*).

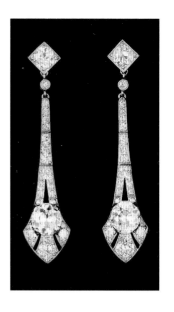

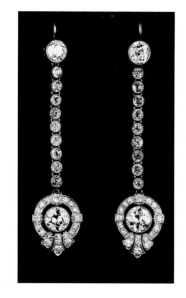

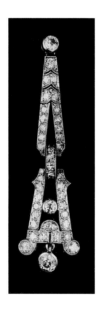

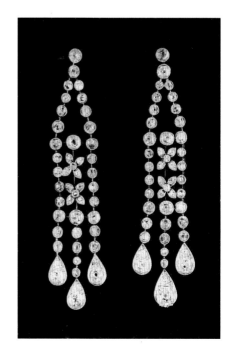

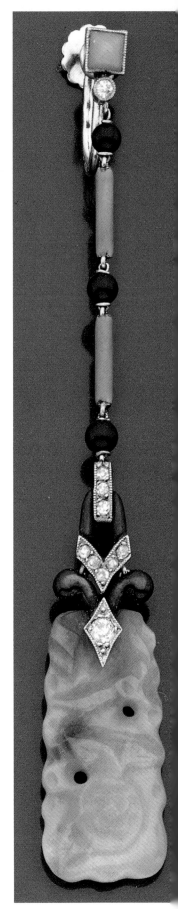

Italian earring set with a carved
red coral drop, suspended on a
contrasting chain with onyx and
diamonds.

Another Italian example
juxtaposing bright colours and
precious and semiprecious stones:
red coral and diamonds.

Gourd-shaped jade drop
suspended from a diamond and
sapphire chain.

Floral panel by Mauboussin,
Paris, also carved in a jade plaque.

THE TRIUMPH OF COLOUR

Rectangular jade plaque imported
from China to form the drop of
the earring, mounted by Liberty,
London.

French emerald and diamond
earrings, the drop designed as a
stylized Chinese lantern.

Earring set throughout with
diamonds in a platinum mount,
representative of the late 1920s
and exceptional for its size.

FLARED DROPS OF
THE LATE TWENTIES

Towards the end of the 1920s earrings
retained their verticality of design but
tended to expand sideways, creating a
greater sense of volume. Instead of
contrasting colours they juxtapose
diamonds of different cuts – brilliants,
baguettes, pear- and fancy-shaped –
mounted next to each other, creating
variety in the play of light and reflection.
The diamond pendent earring by Cartier,
London (*below, second from left*),
designed in 1930, epitomizes this trend.
The motif of the stylized Chinese pagoda
(*right, far right and centre below*)
continues to be exploited as in the early
twenties but it is now adapted to the taste
for more voluminous and wider drops.
Although earrings set entirely with
diamonds were the most common,
coloured gemstones were not disregarded
completely as is testified by the earring by
Drayson, London (*lower left*), set with a
tassel of Indian ruby beads.

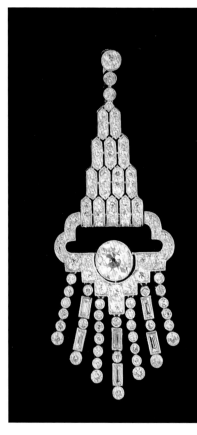

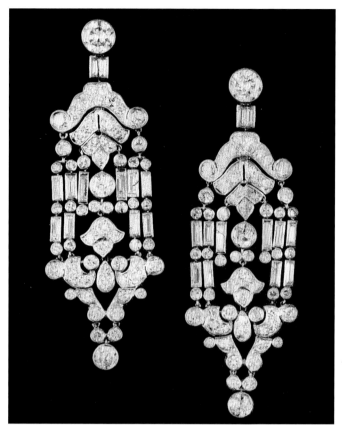

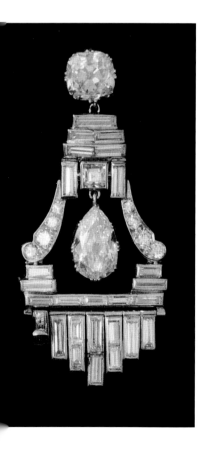

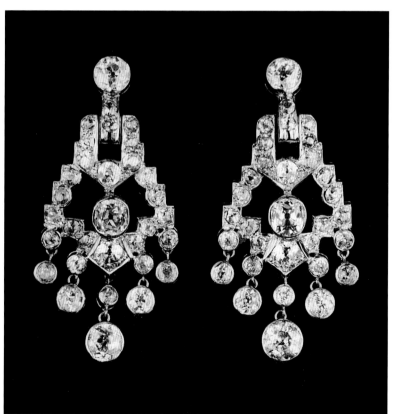

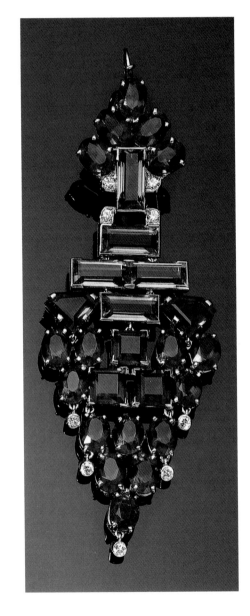

BOLD PENDANTS OF THE THIRTIES

Opposite page:
Though compact earclips were the most common form of earring during the 1930s, long and voluminous pendent earrings were worn for formal evening occasions. A noticeable feature is the return of colour and the exploitation of the different and innovative cuts of the gemstones. Cartier, London, created very successful examples set with rich and voluminous drops mounted with variously cut aquamarines (hexagonal, rectangular, cushion-shaped) of 1933 (*top left*) and (*bottom left*) of 1932, and multicoloured citrines of 1937, enlivened with small pearls and diamonds. In the latter example the use of citrines of various shades of russet and golden yellow anticipates a style typical of the 1940s. The fourth picture shows a late example of the same style, diamond and sapphire bead tassel earrings made by Cartier, Paris, in 1941.

This page:
Three designs for pendent earrings by Cartier, Paris, commissioned by the Maharajah of Patiala in 1935. In 1925 the ruler of Patiala, the largest Sikh state in India, opened his treasury and handed over most of the crown jewels to Cartier for resetting in the fashionable Art Deco style. The commission kept Cartier busy for many years and spurred other Eastern rulers to have their jewels remodelled by famous Parisian jewellers. The three earrings illustrated here successfully combine Indian features such as coloured gemstone beads and bell-shaped forms with the current trend for voluminous pendants set with multicoloured gemstones of different cuts.

ENTER THE CLIP

Clips made their appearance in the early 1930s, and are probably one of the most important innovations in the history of earrings. In the first place the new type of fitting enabled women to wear earrings without piercing their ears, and secondly they allowed, as never before, ornament to be concentrated on the lobe and on the upper part of the ear rather than on the drop. As a result compact designs such as rosettes and spirals, set with concentric lines of diamonds such as the one shown *above* and at times enhanced with coloured gemstones, usually rubies or sapphires, became all the rage. All the examples illustrated show variations of these popular motifs, and it is interesting to note how in many cases the decorative motif curls up, following the ear. For this reason one earclip was designed for the right ear, and the other for the left ear, so that they are not interchangeable. The March 1934 issue of *Femina* (*far right*) advertises, as the fashionable ornament of the time, earclips designed by Boucheron in the shape of *escargots* and *tourbillons*, which envelope the lobe and echo the curls of the hair.

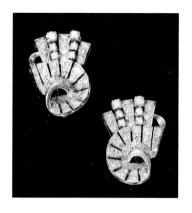

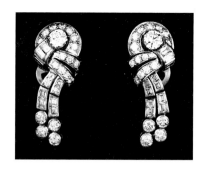

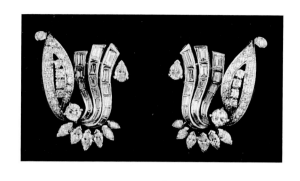

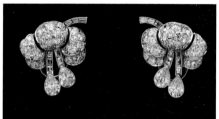

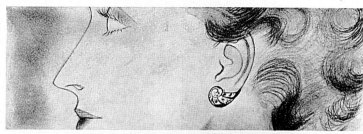

Au-dessus, un clip d'oreille en brillants et diamants baguette. Sa ligne arrondie en forme d'escargot, enveloppe exactement le lobe de l'oreille. C'est le plus charmant bijou qui soit dans sa simplicité.

BIJOUX
1 9 3 4

Et ce sont des bijoux de crise qu'une femme raisonnable peut s'offrir.

Au milieu de la page, un clip de cheveux en brillants, parure délicieuse que nombre de femmes préféreront au trop somptueux diadème. Sur le même profil, on voit un pendant d'oreilles en brillants et rubis que Boucheron dédie plus spécialement aux femmes longues et minces.

En bas, une fantaisie très neuve : le clip "Tourbillon" dont la volute suit un détail de la coiffure et termine celle-ci par le point lumineux de ses brillants et de ses diamants baguette.

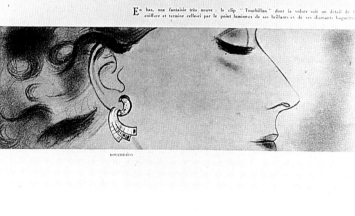

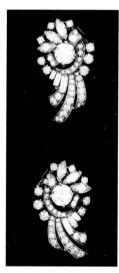

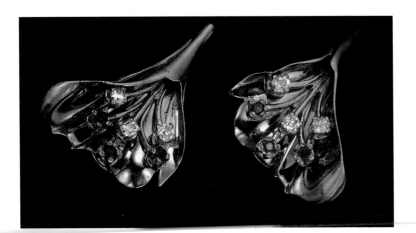

The popular clip of the 1930s continued to be in great favour in the 1940s but diamonds and coloured gemstones were replaced by large surfaces of gold combined with voluminous semiprecious gemstones of moderate intrinsic value and precious stones of small size. A characteristic form was that of scrolled drapes or pleated ribbons rendered with large reflecting surfaces of gold, as in the earclips in white gold, aquamarines, rubies and diamonds by Trabert & Hoeffer, the American branch of Mauboussin (*above left*), circa 1945. Like many other examples of the time, these earclips come with a matching brooch or clip.

The same features are noticeable in the yellow gold, ruby and diamond earclips (*right*). Other earclips of the time favoured naturalistic designs in sharp contrast with the geometrical lines of the previous decade. This is visible in the stylized crocus earclips (*far left*) set with rubies and diamonds within red gold petals and in the gold, ruby and diamond flower (*above*) where the stems curve up to follow the shape of the ear.

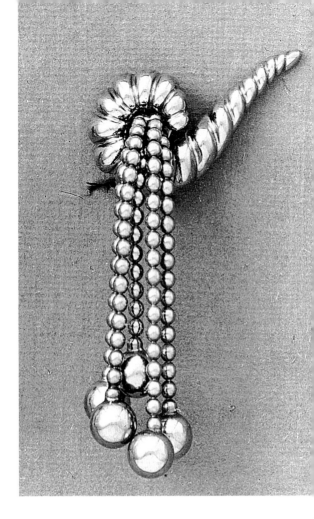

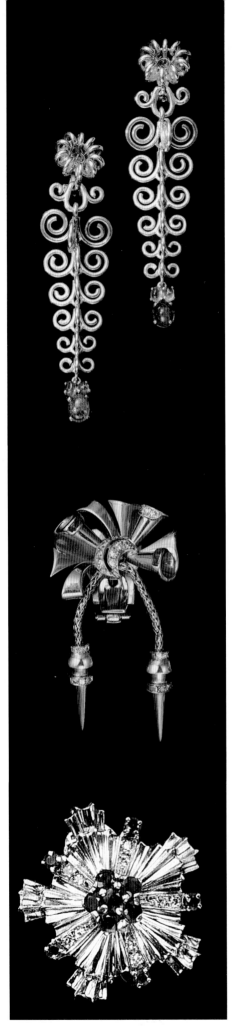

COMPACT CLIP AND
CLIPS WITH PENDANTS
OF THE FORTIES

Although compact clips, such as the ruby, sapphire and diamond flowerhead clusters by Cartier, London, 1945, and the ribbon and flower clip of pierced gold, diamond and rubies (*opposite far right*) or the gold ruby and diamond sunburst earrings by Tiffany (*this page, below right*), were the favoured form of earrings, clips supporting drops and pendants of different nature were also worn. The pendent motifs, however, are merely decorative devices and do not alter the structure which remains that of the fashionable compact clip.

This is the case with the fan-shaped ribbon clip (*this page, centre right*), in gold, rubies and diamonds, which supports two tubular chains with pointed terminals, and with the large step-cut topaz clips (*opposite below*) tied with a similar chain terminating with beaded motifs by Mellerio, 1946. Not dissimilar in spirit are the pair of cornucopia clips by Mellerio, 1947 (*this page, far right*), supporting five beaded chains.

Other examples of pendent earrings are those set with large haematite drops on a gold scroll surmount set with rubies and diamonds (*opposite above*) and the gold and emerald 'Ferronière' pendent earclips, circa 1944, by Mellerio (*this page, top right*).

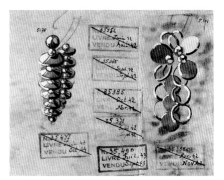

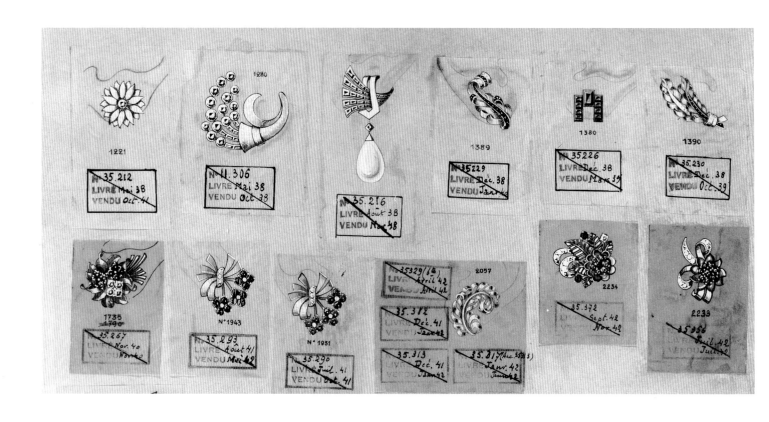

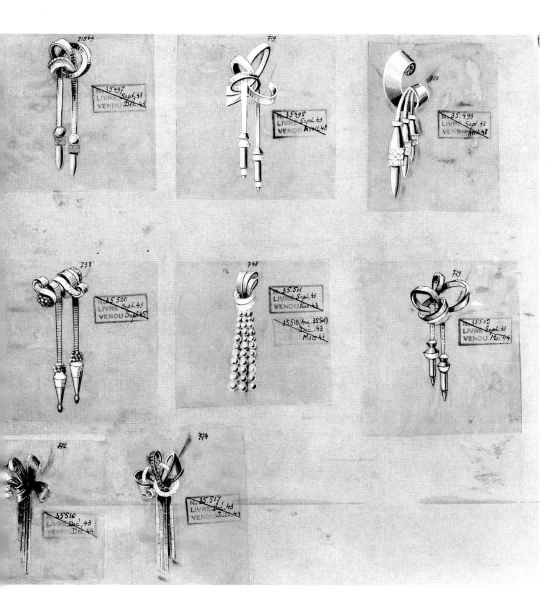

Opposite:

Top centre: Amusing earclips designed as gold and ruby 'jarretières', American, circa 1945, which repeat the design of the very popular 'jarretière' bracelet, and below it a design by Van Cleef & Arpels of the mid-1940s for an amusing and frivolous watch-earring set with *calibré*-cut sapphires.

Right: A gouache design for a earclip by Mauboussin, circa 1945, designed as a ribbon bow with a course of small rubies at the centre: a typical design of the time characterized by wide, unbroken surfaces of gold.

Left: An advertisement in *Vogue* and *Femina* for winter 1945–46 by Boucheron, designed by P. Sim. The model wears a pair of pendent earrings first designed in 1942 in the shape of a cluster of gold discs also illustrated in the archive design below it.

Bottom: A page of earring designs from the Boucheron archives dating from May 1938 to July 1942. Note the transition from the geometrical and platinum set earclips of the late 1930s to the naturalistic motifs such as curled leaves and bouquet of flowers made of gold and coloured gemstones of the 1940s.

This page: Two pages of designs for clips and pendent earrings from the Boucheron archives, mainly of 1943. Although compact clips were the favourite type of ornament, pendent earrings were not completely abandoned. Often the pendent element is very flimsy compared to the bold surmounts consisting of flexible chains terminating with various drops such as cones and beads.

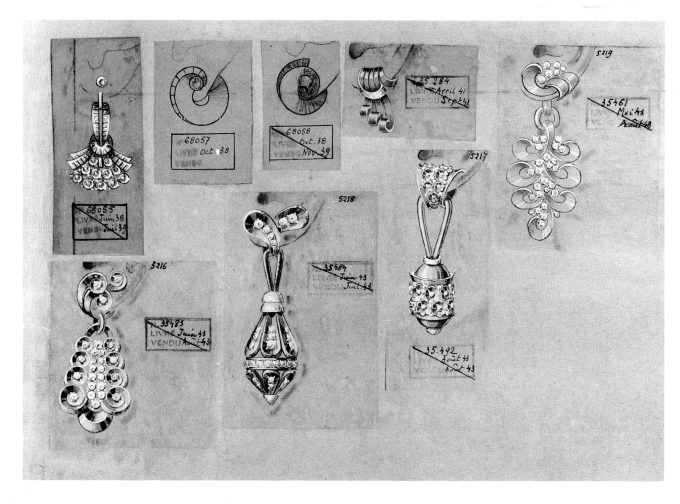

CASCADES OF DIAMONDS

After the war glamorous diamond jewellery came back into fashion – a perfect accessory for the feminine woman of Dior's New Look. Earrings for formal occasions were designed once again with long pendants reminiscent of rainfalls and cascades.

Left: A pair of diamond pendent earrings mounted in platinum of the 1950s, by Van Cleef & Arpels, New York, designed as a turban surmount supporting a cascade of baguette diamonds with pear-shaped drops. Note the emphasis on the fluidity and movement conveyed by the continuous line of baguette diamonds.

Right: A diamond pendent earring by Mellerio, 1952; the knotted surmount supports a tassel of baguettes and brilliant-cut diamonds.

Below: A collection of pendent earrings and earclips of 1952 by Mellerio. Rosettes, stylized leaves and pendent tassels set with diamonds were among the most popular motifs for earrings.

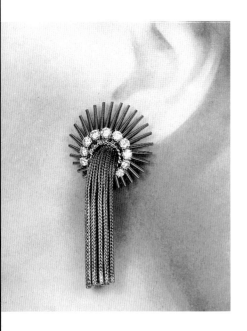

Top row: Gold and diamond tassel earclips by Van Cleef & Arpels, circa 1950, characterized by an innovative use of gold worked into *passementerie* effects.

Centre row: A collection of pendent earrings of the 1950s all set with diamonds of various cuts, the emphasis being placed on the fluidity of the lines and the richness of the material.

Bottom row, in order. First: A pair of cultured pearl and diamond earrings designed as fuchsia blossoms, a model popular with Van Cleef & Arpels since the late 1940s. *Second:* A pair of cultured pearl and diamond earrings, 1989, by Verdura, based on an original Verdura design of 1953. Note the detachable drops set respectively with a black and a white pearl. *Third and fourth:* Two pairs of earrings, combining pearl drops with entwined ribbons or flowerspray surmounts set with diamonds of various cuts.

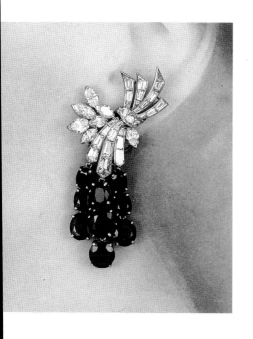

GOLD, PEARL AND DIAMOND GLAMOUR
OF THE FIFTIES

During the 1950s there came to be a marked distinction between day and evening jewellery; the former made of gold and set with coloured gemstones or small diamonds, the latter of platinum, or other white metal, and set preferably with diamonds and pearls.

Left: A gold, turquoise and diamond earring mounted with a tassel of gold chains supporting turquoise beads, one of the popular coloured gemstones of the period.

Far left: A diamond and sapphire pendent earring, by Van Cleef & Arpels, circa 1950. Though diamonds were the favourite stones for important earrings, coloured precious gemstones were at times introduced to enliven the monochromatic effect of diamond spray and cascade motifs.

Both long and short earrings enjoyed great popularity in the 1960s, exploiting the different textures of materials, bright colours and abstract forms.

Below: Two pairs of gold and diamond pendent earrings by Meister, respectively late 1960s and 1971. Both show settings based on natural forms – mimosa blossom and sea-urchin.

Above: A pair of shell pendent earrings with 'elephant tusk' shells within a cagework of gold wire on a gold rosette surmount, by Andrew Grima, circa 1968.

Opposite:
Top left: A pair of gold, turquoise and green *plique-à-jour* enamel and diamond earclips by Marit Aschan, 1966.

Top right: A pair of dioptase, sapphire and diamond pendent earrings, mounted in gold, mid-1960s.

Centre: A pair of gold and sapphire earclips by Enrico Serafini, mid-1960s, designed as knotted roots. And a pair of gold, red coral and diamond earclips, by Sterlé, 1960s; the jagged mounts suggest the idea of a mass of 'frozen' molten metal.

Bottom left: A pair of gold, emerald and ruby earclips, Italian, 1960s. The amoeba-like abstract design combines typical features of the time: the large cabochon emerald, textured gold mount and striking use of colour.

Bottom centre and right: Two pairs of earclips by Arthur King, 1960s, respectively set with red coral and cultured pearls and diamonds within gold borders reminiscent of sprawling roots.

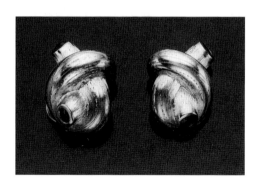

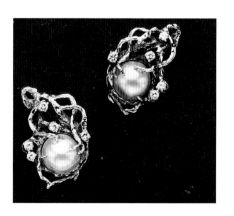

THE COLOURFUL SIXTIES

Above: A collection of shell earclips set in gold, two mounted with coral and turquoise, of the mid-1960s. Typical is the interest in unusual textures and colour combinations and in materials not necessarily of high intrinsic value. Jewellers such as David Webb and Verdura of New York and Darde et Fils of Paris transformed exotic and colourful shells into very attractive earclips. All those shown here belonged to the Duchess of Windsor.

Right: A pair of onyx and ruby earclips by Schlumberger, 1968, designed as stylized pineapples. It is during this period that amusing and 'surrealistic' subjects became fashionable motifs for earrings.

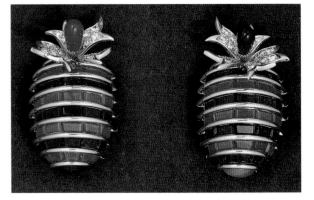

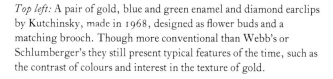

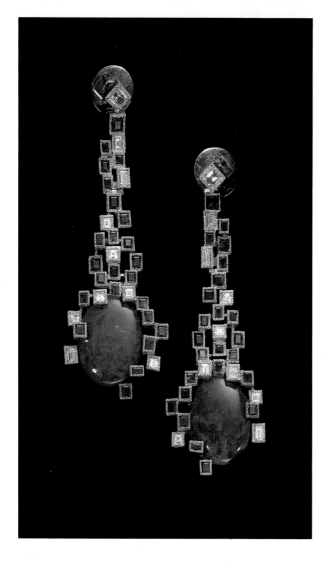

Top left: A pair of gold, blue and green enamel and diamond earclips by Kutchinsky, made in 1968, designed as flower buds and a matching brooch. Though more conventional than Webb's or Schlumberger's they still present typical features of the time, such as the contrast of colours and interest in the texture of gold.

Top right: Pair of surrealistic earclips by Salvador Dali, mid-1950s, designed as a pair of honeycomb hearts set with rubies and diamonds. Surrealistic themes which appeared in jewellery in the 1950s became fashionable and widely accepted in the 1960s.

Right: A pair of opal, emerald sapphire and diamond pendent earrings mounted in gold, by Andrew Grima, 1966, typical of the time in their abstract design, interest in different textures and vivid contrasting colours. These earrings won the Duke of Edinburgh Prize for Elegant Design in 1966.

Above: Another Dali earclip of the 1950s, of winged design, inscribed with the artist's name in black enamel.

IMAGES OF THE EIGHTIES

Left: Four pairs of earclips set with diamonds in yellow gold, and one pair set with haematites designed by Bulgari, 1985–88. Typically their design is bold and fairly compact and the diamonds are all set in yellow gold. The *Parenthesis* motif on the half-hoop earclips of 1985 which consists of a gold reeded decoration suggesting brackets (hence the name) has become a trademark of Bulgari.

Below left: A pair of star-shaped citrine, onyx, small diamonds and sapphire earclips by Bulgari, reflecting the fashion for decorative and fairly large compact earclips set with colourful materials not necessarily of very high intrinsic value. The cut of the stones is conditioned by the design, both sapphire and citrines being cut to fit the hexagonal collets.

Opposite: Eight designs for earrings made by Marina B between 1983 and 1989, with the actual realization of two of them – a pair of grey and white mabe pearl *Pneus* earrings designed in 1981, and a pair of yellow gold, black steel and diamond *Kin* earrings of 1987. However varied the forms and materials, they show the same boldness and three-dimensional quality. *Carmen* is set with diamonds, green agate, onyx and a golden citrine drop inset with a burnt citrine; *Cimin* with blue topazes, pink tourmalines, amethysts, citrines and burnished gold; the hoop of *Funny* is characterized by a yellow gold lattice on a black metal base.

EC. LORETO

EC. GOAR.

EC. CARMEN

EC. ALEXIA

EC. NAJWA

EC. CIMIN

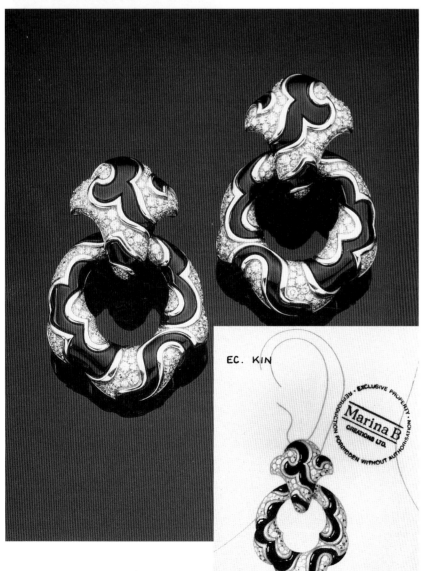

EC. KIN

EC. FUNNY

DIAMONDS AND GOLD IN
THE EIGHTIES

To give small diamonds a setting of yellow gold can create an effect that is subtler but just as glamorous as using coloured gemstones.

Opposite, from top to bottom: A pair of earclips by Repossi made in the 1980s, twisted hoops decorated with bands of pavé-set diamonds alternating with yellow gold; a pair of yellow gold and diamond earclips of the 1980s retailed by Harry Winston, Geneva, and made of hammered yellow gold inset with pear-shaped diamonds; and a pair of *Ecume* earclips designed by Marina B in 1984, mounted in yellow gold with pavé-set small brilliant-cut diamonds arranged in wave-like patterns.

Above, from left to right: A pair of lozenge-shaped earclips made in the 1980s, the black onyx plaques with diamond borders set at the centre with aquamarines cut with buff-tops; a pair of *Pivopoire* pendent earclips, designed in 1986 by Marina B, the surmounts set with green tourmalines and diamonds supporting a large faceted pink quartz drop; and a pair of rock crystal onyx and diamonds *Pneus* pendent earrings, also by Marina. B.

Right: Three earrings by Bulgari of 1988 and 1989. The first has a cabochon emerald in a border of *calibré*-cut emerald and rubies and small brilliant-cut diamonds; the second is set with a combination of emerald, rubies and sapphires and diamonds mounted in yellow gold; and the third is a gold, amethyst, pink tourmaline, peridot and blue topaz earring. Note the colourful effect of the cabochon stones.

Two more pairs of Bulgari earclips, one with diamond-set cushion-shaped panels decorated with stylized flowers and leaves of pink sapphires and emeralds, the other set with multicoloured sugar-loaf cabochon gemstones mounted in yellow gold.

THE ELONGATED HOOP OF THE SEVENTIES

Elongated oval hoops carved in semiprecious hardstone such as onyx, coral, and lapis lazuli, frequently highlighted with diamond-set motifs, were popular for day wear. *Left:* A pair of onyx and diamond pendent earrings, by Mauboussin, 1973.

Opposite: A collection of designs for earrings of the seventies by Boucheron, mostly repeating the fashionable motif of the hoop pendant on a similarly shaped surmount. There is great variety in the choice of materials: differently textured gold, brightly coloured enamel and various gemstones and hardstones such as cabochon emeralds, lapis lazuli, coral, tiger's eye. The favourite model appears to be the elongated drop-shaped hoop on a similarly designed surmount placed upside-down in relation to the drop; this particular design of 1970, *Créole,* is repeated five times in various colours. It is interesting to note the orientalizing design of the 1978 pendent earring (*centre, far right*).

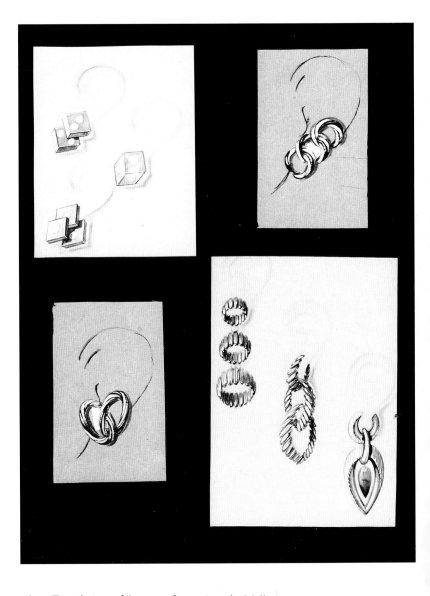

Above: Four designs of the 1970s for earrings, by Mellerio. The first, top left, with gold and diamond-set dice continues the 1960s fashion for surrealism. *Left:* A pair of diamond and yellow gold pendent earrings made by M. Gérard in 1978–79.

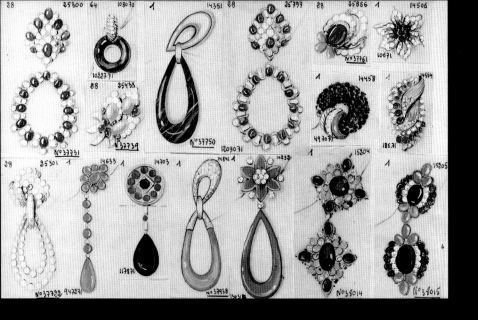

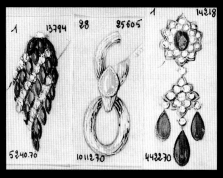

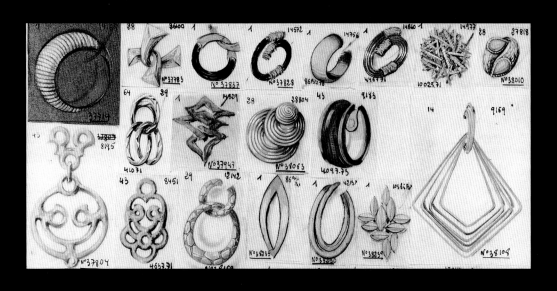

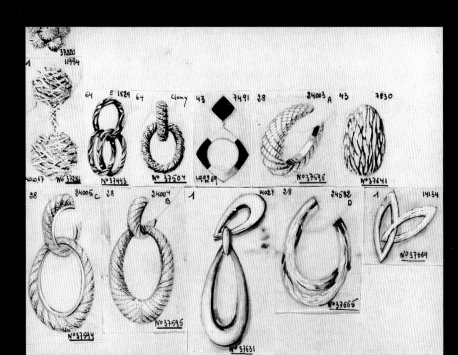

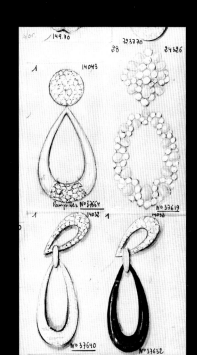

ANTIQUITY IN VOGUE

It is Bulgari who since the mid-1970s has led the way in the use of coins in earrings. On this page they are all ancient Greek and Roman except those right centre (Neapolitan, 1680) and bottom centre (Dutch Indies, 1719–40). One of the features of these earrings is the combination of ancient materials with sleek modern mounts.

Right: A pair of 18 carat matt gold earclips by Lalaounis created in the 1980s. The rams' head terminal recalls late Classical Greek prototypes, and the use of matt 18 carat gold is an attempt to match the colour and texture of the ancient examples.

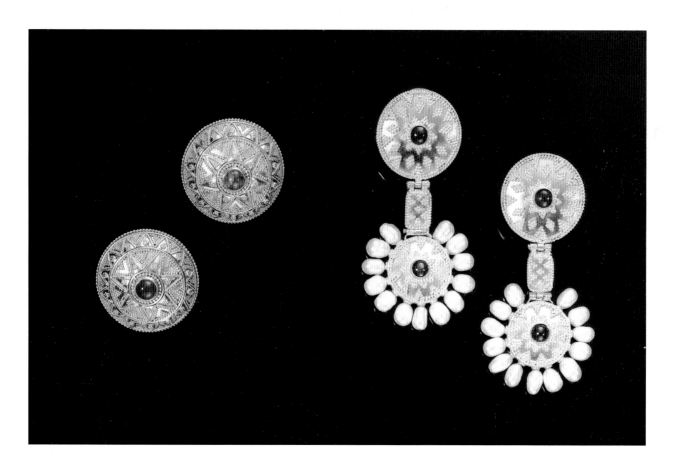

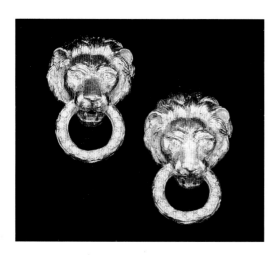

Above: Two pairs of gold earrings respectively decorated with emeralds and rubies in a border of pearls, by Lalaounis, 1980s. In this case the source of inspiration is not Classical antiquity but Byzantium.

Left: A pair of gold earclips designed as a lion mask supporting a hoop, a pastiche of antique elements rather than an imitation of an ancient prototype. The motif of the lion mask has been successfully exploited by most of the important jewellers throughout Europe and the United States.

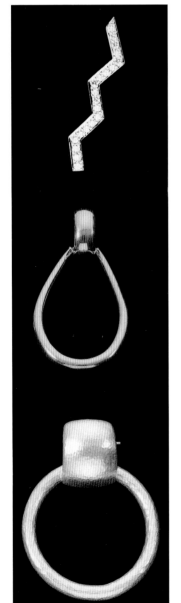

GOLD REFLECTION
OF THE EIGHTIES

The fashion for large and bold earrings of
sculptural effect whose impact relies on the rich
colour of gold, its texture and reflective qualities
is well exemplified by the creations of Paloma
Picasso and Elsa Peretti for Tiffany.

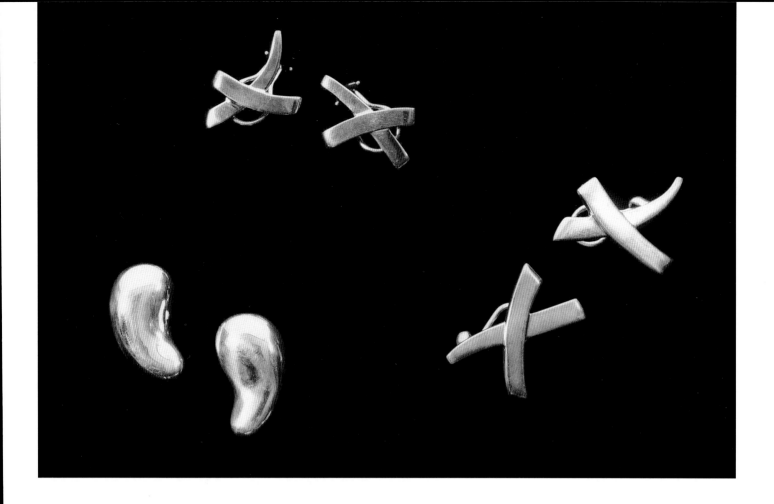

Above: Two pairs of gold 'kiss' earclips by Paloma Picasso for Tiffany, designed in 1988 and a pair of gold 'bean' earclips by Elsa Peretti for Tiffany, first designed in 1974, which have gained great popularity in the last decade.

Below: A group of earpieces comprising: a diamond stud, two molten gold and diamond discs and an earpiece consisting of a circular matt topaz and an elongated molten gold plaque by Gerda Flockinger, 1986. An unusual feature is the possibility given by these four elements to create various different combinations as pairs. The interest in textured gold developed in the 1960s and continued to be exploited successfully until the 1980s. Note here the combination of molten effect, wire-work and granulation.

Opposite
Top: Sterling silver, free form bean earrings by Elsa Peretti designed exclusively for Tiffany, 1974, and a whip belt en suite.

Far left: A gold and diamond 'Thunderbolt' earring by Paloma Picasso for Tiffany, designed in 1988, and two hammered gold hoop earrings by Paloma Picasso for Tiffany, designed in 1989.

Below right: Pair of gold hoop earrings and drop ball earrings by Paloma Picasso, designed exclusively for Tiffany, 1989. The simple lines of hoops and bosses are close in spirit to the archaeological examples illustrated on pp. 25 and 32.

THE GLAMOUR OF DIAMONDS

It is only since the last decades that elaborate and decorative mounts have gone out of fashion, leaving exceptional stones mounted in very simple and unobtrusive claw-settings. The perfection of the stone, whether a pure white diamond or a coloured gemstone, is the essence of these creations and design is clearly subordinated to the gem.

Right: A pair of diamond earrings by Harry Winston designed as a flexible garland of foliate motifs set with navette-, pear-shaped and brilliant-cut diamonds. In spite of the fact that the stones are fairly small, their quality and match is exceptional.

Centre row: A pair of pear-shaped diamond earrings; a pair of pear-shaped diamond earrings with marquise-shaped diamond foliate motifs; and a pair of pure white (D colour) diamond earrings, by Harry Winston, each set with a cluster of pear-shaped diamonds supporting pear-shaped drops weighing respectively 34.80 cts and 37.12 cts. Note how the platinum claws are kept to the minimum.

Bottom: A pair of fancy yellow diamond earclips, set with step-cut and pear-shaped diamonds; a pair of diamond pendent earrings, the two pear-shaped stones weighing respectively 5.07 and 5.01 cts, D flawless on pear-shaped diamond surmounts weighing 23 cts in total, mounted in platinum; and a pair of brilliant-cut diamond earrings, the larger stones weighing 27.15 cts and 28.13 cts.

Opposite top: A pair of diamond cluster earclips by Harry Winston set with a combination of marquise- and pear-shaped stones. A trademark of the firm not only in the design but also in the quality of the gemstones (51.22 cts of D flawless stones)..

Opposite bottom: A pair of hoop ruby and diamond earrings by David Webb, a precious interpretation of a simple design which is as old as the history of earrings.

Earrings designed by Graff in 1989, with two perfectly
matched D flawless heart-shaped diamonds of 63.3 cts
suspended from similar quality pear-shaped stones
totalling 26.44 cts. The rarity and value of these
earrings derives both from the quality of the gemstones
and the difficulty of matching them in perfect pairs.

Biographical notes on designers
Glossary
Bibliography
Acknowledgments
Index

Biographical notes on designers

Aschan, Marit

Marit Guinness Aschan lives and works in her studio in Chelsea, London. She was born in London of an Irish father and a Norwegian mother. Having left school at the age of 15, she began her training as a painter first in Munich, Florence and Paris and then in London. In the 1950s she began working with the medium of enamel, which because of its unique translucent properties inspired her to render the shifting effects and colour of sky and sea on both large and small scale objects. She has been able to fire up to thirty different layers of enamel on one single piece of metal, when five are usually considered sufficient. She has also developed the technique of *plique-à-jour* enamel – a method in which there is no metal base to back the enamel, so that light may shine through, like a stained glass window. Marit Aschan has devised a way of twisting lengths of wire into a honeycomb of cells rather than soldering little strips of metal or piercing a solid sheet of metal in the traditional fashion of *plique-à-jour*.

Among her most important commissions are the central enamel for Louis Osman's High Altar Cross for Exeter Cathedral and the binding for *The Great Houses of Europe* for J.R. Abbey. Jewels have won Marit Aschan special recognition. A brooch and a pair of earrings in *plique-à-jour* translucent enamel randomly set with diamonds were purchased by the Worshipful Company of Goldsmiths London for their permanent collection; and were shown in five major museums of art throughout the United States in 1966–67 on the occasion of the exhibition 'Five Centuries of Treasures from the Worshipful Company of Goldsmiths London'. In 1971 she was one of the select few contemporary enamellists to be included in the exhibition 'A Thousand Years of Enamel' at Wartski's.

As one of the most distinguished enamellists of our time Marit Aschan has been President of the society of Artist Enamellers since its foundation in 1958. Her work is signed with her initials: MGA.

Bapst

The oldest family of Parisian jewellers. They came originally from Swabia in Southern Germany and became prominent in France making court jewellery. The business was started in Paris in 1725 and flourished throughout the 18th century. In 1797 Jacques-Eberhard Bapst (1771–1841) married Marie-Nicole Ménière, daughter of the Parisian court jeweller Paul-Nicolas Ménière, and taking the name Bapst-Ménière became court jeweller under the Restoration. Between 1814 and 1820 he remounted Napoleon's jewels for Louis XVIII, and in 1825 he completed the crown and sword for the coronation of Charles X. As a consequence of the political events of 1848 the post of Crown Jeweller was abolished, but the firm, under the direction of Charles Bapst, joined by his nephew Alfred, the son of his brother Constant, continued to do business under the name of Bapst et neveu. When Charles Bapst died in 1871, it was carried on by Alfred and by his two cousins Jules and Paul Bapst. Alfred Bapst was a very talented jewellery designer and to his hand must be ascribed most of the parures which were remounted for the Empress Eugénie. After his death in 1879 his son Germain Bapst joined Lucien Falize while Jules and Paul Bapst, together with Jules's son Armand, started in 1880 a new 'maison' in Faubourg-Saint-Honoré and traded under the name J. and P. Bapst and Son.

Belperron Suzanne (1899–1983)

French-born Suzanne Belperron moved to Paris to study at the Ecole des Beaux-Arts, where she learnt and developed her ability to draw and design. In 1918 she began designing for the Parisian jeweller René Boivin. She collaborated with Boivin for approximately a decade and then in 1933 she began designing for Bernard Herz, one of the most important pearl merchants of the time. During the war Bernard Herz was deported and in 1945 Suzanne Belperron joined in partnership with his son Jean Herz; the firm with premises at 59 Rue de Châteaudun came to be known as Herz-Belperron. Jean Herz was in charge of its financial and commercial aspect, while Suzanne Belperron looked after the artistic side of the business. The jewels she designed were characterized by bold and pure lines, devoid of superfluous adornment, matt and shiny surfaces. Precious and semiprecious materials were frequently juxtaposed such as frosted rock crystal and diamonds, stained blue chalcedony and sapphires. The firm did not have an inhouse workshop so most of Belperron's designs were executed by the highly skilled Parisian workshop of Groene et Darde. Suzanne Belperron refused to produce an item which was not perfect in every way and it was not uncommon for her to return a jewel to Groene et Darde because it did not meet her standards.

Though shunning the commercial world Suzanne Belperron's renown was soon well established on both sides of the Atlantic. Until the end of her life Suzanne Belperron continued to design striking jewels which she never signed, for she argued that her style and jewels did not need a signature to identify them. Usually, a clue of authenticity of Belperron jewels is provided by fitted cases stamped Herz-Belperron or the maker's mark for Groene et Darde.

Boucheron

The firm Boucheron was founded in 1858 by Frédéric Boucheron. He opened a shop in the Palais-Royal, an area which housed numerous Parisian jewellers. He rapidly gained recognition and success, and in 1867, the first time he exhibited in Paris, he won a gold medal. Later he won the first prize at the Philadelphia exhibition in 1875. Following this success, the French government in 1876 granted him the cross of the Légion d'Honneur, and at the Paris exhibition in 1889 he was awarded another first prize and the cross of officer of the Légion d'Honneur. More prizes followed in 1900. In 1893 Boucheron moved to 26 Place Vendôme, the firm's present premises and formerly the residence of the Countess of Castiglione, one of the favourites of Napoleon III. Frédéric Boucheron was the first jeweller to move to this square which has since become the world's centre for haute joaillerie.

In 1902 Boucheron opened a branch in Moscow which closed at the beginning of the Russian Revolution in 1917. After Frédéric's death in 1902 the firm was headed by his son Louis, who continued the firm's policy of expansion abroad. In 1903 he opened a branch in London at 180 New Bond Street where it still remains today, and founded Boucheron Company Incorporated in New York. He continued to take part in numerous international exhibitions – Liège, Milan, Madrid, Saragossa, Brussels – and the firm continued to reap medals and prizes. In 1930 Louis Boucheron was summoned to Teheran by Reza Shah Pahlavi to value the 'Thousand and One Nights Treasure' which stood as security for the currency of Iran. He was then nominated official expert and guardian of the treasure. After 1936 Louis Boucheron was assisted in the directorship of the firm by his two sons Gérard and Fred and since the 70s the firm has been headed by Gérard's son Alain.

During the firm's successful 130 years of business it has built up and continues to increase its list of illustrious patrons: the Maharaja of Patiala, the Imperial Family of Iran, the Royal

Family of Saudi Arabia, the Begum Aga Khan, members of the British Royal Family, the Sultan of Brunei, Princess Caroline of Monaco and a number of personalities from the world of entertainment. In recent years Boucheron has increased also its number of sales points. A start was made in Japan where six shops were opened in 1973; another shop was opened in Geneva in 1982 and in Gstaad in 1986, Hong Kong in 1988 and Milan and Cannes in 1989. In 1988 Boucheron held a retrospective exhibition at the Musée Jacquemart-André, in Paris to mark the firm's 130th anniversary. In recent years Boucheron has launched a perfume created as a jewel with its bottle in the shape of a ring.

Boucheron's jewels have always combined a high quality of workmanship and design. Recently the firm has created jewels set with rock crystal combined with precious gems. Boucheron jewels are mainly signed: Boucheron (the initial B in gothic character).

Brogden, John (working 1842–1885)

A London jeweller and goldsmith, partner of the firm Watherston and Brogden from 1842 to 1864 when he took over the premises at 16 Henrietta Street, Covent Garden, and continued to run the business independently under his own name until 1880. His work was mainly in the antique styles: Assyrian and Egyptian motifs were among his favourites, but themes from classical archaeology and the French or Italian Renaissance were also exploited. He exhibited at the London and Paris exhibitions of 1851, 1855, 1862, 1867 and in 1878 his archaeological pieces at the Paris Exposition Universelle impressed Castellani. John Brogden signed his pieces with the monogram JB or his surname in full.

Bulgari

A leading Italian jewellery firm of Greek origin, founded by Sotirio Bulgari, a skilled silversmith renowned for renewing the ancient local tradition of engraving. Sotirio emigrated to Naples in 1879, and finally settled in Rome where he opened his first shop in Via Sistina in 1884. Twenty years later he opened another shop in Via Condotti (a shop that still remains the flagship of the firm), and was joined in the business by his sons Costantino and Giorgio. After a long time spent in France, Giorgio dedicated his life to creating a 'Bulgari style' in gold and silver. His brother Costantino embodied years of research and study in the reference book *Argentieri, Orafi e Gemmari d'Italia*, an authoritative work on the Italian art of goldsmithry. After World War II sons and nephews continued in the family tradition and Bulgari acquired international fame. In the 1960s the first shops outside Italy were opened: in New York, Paris, Geneva and Monte Carlo. In the 1980s more Bulgari shops opened in Europe: London, Milan, Munich, St Moritz; and in the Far East: Singapore, Hong Kong, Osaka and Tokyo, culminating in November 1989 with the opening of a second showroom in New York on Fifth Avenue.

Today the firm is run by Giorgio's sons Paolo and Nicola, and their nephew Francesco Trapani is Managing Director. Bulgari jewels are usually signed with the full name of the firm in Roman capitals: BVLGARI.

Cartier

The firm was first established by Louis-François Cartier (1819–1904), who served his apprenticeship with Adolph Picard, at 29 Rue Montargueil, Paris, in 1847; the firm soon distinguished itself for originality and soundness of taste. In 1853 the workshop was transferred to 5 Rue Neuve-des-Petits-Champs and business quickly prospered with the support of important clients such as the Countess of Nieuwerkerke, Princess Mathilde, cousin of Napoleon III, and the Empress Eugénie.

In 1859 the business again moved to larger premises at 9 Boulevard des Italiens, producing jewels of exceptional taste but modest size: small emeralds, amethysts, pearls and garnets set in silver and gold. The firm also offered simple silver objects, ivories and bronzes. The business was run on patriarchal principles, with Louis-François Cartier at the head and his son Alfred (1841–1925) in charge of the gemstones. An expert in precious gemstones, talented artist and astute businessman, Alfred Cartier was soon recognized throughout Europe.

Following the French defeat at Sedan in 1870, the disruptive policies of the Commune ruined the Cartier business. Alfred Cartier sought refuge in England and temporarily established his business in London. In 1874 he took over his father's business in Paris with the intention of reestablishing the firm under the 3rd Republic. Cartier continued to sell all sorts of objects: fans, bronzes, ivories, Wedgwood medallions, silverware, Sèvres porcelain and, of course, jewellery and watches. Its clientèle was, by now, a combination of aristocratic families and well-off members of the middle classes, including bankers and industrialists.

In 1898 the firm moved to 13 Rue de la Paix, next door to the premises of the world's most famous couturiers of the time, Jean-Philippe and Gaston Worth. The marriage of Alfred Cartier's son Louis (1875–1942) to Andrée Worth brought the two firms in close contact working for the same clientèle.

The new premises were formally inaugurated in November 1899, and the move happened to coincide with the introduction of a new kind of platinum jewellery in the fashionable 'garland style'. Louis Cartier and his brother Pierre (1878–1965) used this as a pretext for drawing the attention of the world's aristocracy and royal families to the new premises. The Prince of Wales, the future Edward VII, who had become a close friend of Alfred and Louis Cartier, commissioned 27 diadems for his coronation in 1902.

The same year Pierre Cartier set up a branch in London, at 4 New Burlington Street. The premises were transferred to 175 New Bond Street in 1909, and their direction given to Jacques Cartier (1884–1942), the youngest of the family. The first certificate of royal appointment was bestowed in 1904 by King Edward VII, followed by the warrants of King Alfonso XIII of Spain and King Carlos of Portugal. Maharajas and oriental princes started to become fervent admirers of Cartier's art and style.

Under the guidance of Louis Cartier the firm prospered creating splendid jewels, works of art, wristwatches and clocks for the rich and famous. In 1908 the opening of a branch in New York was the response to the American economic boom.

Diamond dog collars, devant de corsages, lavallières and tiaras in the 'garland style' set in platinum were produced at Cartier to complement the fashions of the time. The First World War put an end to the 'Belle Epoque', but Louis Cartier foresaw how different women would be after the war, and as early as 1916 he began tracing the lines of a new style of jewellery which would suit the dynamic and slender women of the 1920s. The 1925 Paris Exhibition of Decorative Arts confirmed Cartier's supremacy in jewellery and watchmaking. Louis Cartier was supported by excellent collaborators such as Charles Jacqueau, Jeanne Toussaint and Peter Lemarchand. In 1933 he handed over the responsibilities of the high jewellery department to Jeanne Toussaint, who created an extremely successful line in yellow gold and coloured stones. In 1935 Cartier opened a branch in Cannes and later, in 1938, also one in Monte Carlo and one in Palm Beach.

During the difficult times of the Second World War, it was Jeanne Toussaint and her team who assumed responsibility for the Rue de la Paix business, while Pierre and Louis Cartier were in New York and Jacques in St Moritz. Louis Cartier and his younger brother Jacques died within six months in 1942. Jacques Cartier's son Jean-Jacques assumed responsibility for New Bond Street. Louis Cartier's son Claude managed Cartier Paris for a few months in 1946 before returning to New York. Paris became the fief of Pierre Claudel, Pierre Cartier's son-in-law. During the following decades responsibilities were transferred and finally Paris, London and New York were assigned to different groups. In 1970 a branch was opened in Geneva and one in Hong Kong; in 1971 another was opened in Munich.

In 1972 Robert Hocq became president of Cartier Paris. In co-operation with Alain Perrin he established the doctrine of 'Les Must de Cartier' which enabled Must Boutiques, selling jewels at more affordable prices, to be opened around the world. In 1973 a branch was opened in Tokyo, and in the same year Robert Hocq acquired the management of Cartier London and entrusted to his daughter Nathalie the responsibility for high fashion jewellery and the supervision together with Alain Perrin of the gold jewels designed for the 'Must' collection. Robert Hocq took over the management of Cartier New York in 1978.

Cartier sign their pieces with the name in script or block capitals, usually followed by the name or the names of the Paris, London and New York branches. For the marks used by the firm see: Hans Nadelhoffer, *Cartier, Jewelers Extraordinary*, 1984.

Castellani

The Castellani firm was started in Rome in 1814 by Fortunato Pio Castellani (1794–1865). It is known that the early years of his production are characterized by jewels in the contemporary French, English, Swiss and Russian taste, but there is no means of identifying them because of their conventional and derivative nature, and because they were not signed with the typical monogram consisting of two entwined Cs characteristic of the later production in archaeological revival taste.

During the 1820s Fortunato Pio Castellani, himself a jeweller and an antique dealer, became progressively more interested in Etruscan jewellery through his friendship with the famous archaeologist Michelangelo Caetani. Caetani persuaded Fortunato Pio, by then joined in his business by two of his sons, Alessandro (1824–1883) and Augusto (1829–1914), to abandon jewellery in contemporary European taste, and concentrate on jewels of antique and archaeological inspiration. The Castellanis not only used antiquity as a source of inspiration, but also studied and revived the goldsmith techniques of the past, and concentrated on the difficult task of rediscovering the secret of Etruscan granulation, achieving good results, probably working with a technique similar to that used by the Etruscans.

Castellani's replicas and creations were based on original pieces such as those found in excavation of Cerveteri, Vulci, Chiusi, Orvieto and Tarquinia. In addition the Castellanis, linked by close bonds of friendship to the Cavalier Campana, the director of the Sacro Monte di Pietà di Roma, helped and directed him in the formation of his important collection of works of art which included hundreds of Greek, Etruscan and Roman jewels. This put them in the very privileged position of marketing commercial pastiches based on the Campana collection originals, and becoming famous throughout Europe as revivalist jewellers. The Castellani production is celebrated for jewels in Greek, Roman and Etruscan taste, often set with Roman mosaic plaques or mounted with antique intaglios or coins. In the late 1860s they extended the archaeological production to include Byzantine and Merovingian styles.

When Fortunato Pio died in 1865, the Rome workshop passed to Augusto, a keen classical historian and honorary director of the Musei Capitolini. The original shop of Via del Corso was moved in 1853 to Via Poli, and from there to 86 Piazza Fontana di Trevi in 1881. The business operated there until 1930, quietly run by Augusto's son Alfredo (1853–1930) on the good reputation of his forebears.

Alessandro, who had lost an arm in a hunting accident in 1837, never took an active part in the production side of the business apart from designing jewellery. As a consequence of his liberal and republican ideals he was imprisoned for political reasons between 1853 and 1856, and subsequently banished from Rome. In 1860 he fled to Paris where thanks to his connections with Michelangelo Caetani, he was introduced into the fashionable and cultural salons of the time. Whilst in Paris, he dealt with the acquisition by the French government of the famous Campana collection when the Cavalier Campana, accused of maladministration, was forced to sell it by Papal order. The exhibition of the Campana collection at the Louvre produced a great impact on the public and soon became a source of inspiration for many jewellers such as Eugène Fontenay, whose antiquarian interest urged him to revive the archaeological styles. In 1863 Alessandro opened the Castellani workshop in Naples and left its management to the gifted Neapolitan goldsmith and jeweller Giacinto Melillo.

The Castellanis almost invariably marked their pieces. Three types of Castellani marks are known: the first monogram consisting of two entwined Cs, is set at the centre of a cartouche-shaped motif; the second mark consists of the simple monogram; the third and rarest mark consists of the monogram ACC which is possibly associated only with the work of Alessandro Castellani.

Civilotti, Antonio (1798–1870)
A Roman jeweller and goldsmith renowned for his work in archaeological and Renaissance revival styles. In 1830 he first established his premises at 128 Via del Corso, and in 1857 moved to 18 Via dei Canestrari where he remained until 1870.

Flockinger, Gerda
Gerda Flockinger was born in Innsbruck, Austria in 1927. She studied fine arts at St Martin's School, London between 1945 and 50, and then etching, jewellery and enamelling at the Central School of Art and Design in London from 1950 to 1955. She taught from 1962–68 at the Hornsey College of Art in London where she created a modern jewellery course. Gerda Flockinger's gold and silver jewels are all one-off and are characterized by a special technique of fusing the metal rather than soldering it. Her work has been extensively exhibited both in group and in solo exhibitions such as those of 1971 and 1986 at the Victoria and Albert Museum in London. Her work is also featured in numerous public collections such as the City of Bristol Museum and Art Gallery, Bristol; Royal Museum of Scotland, Edinburgh; The Worshipful Company of Goldsmiths, London; Crafts Council, London; Victoria and Albert Museum, London; Castle Museum, Nottingham and Schmuckmuseum, Pforzheim. Flockinger's jewels are most commonly signed: they have a small disc bearing her initials GF, and from 1986 an additional disc stamped with a flowerhead.

Fontenay, Eugène (1823–1887)
Eugène Fontenay was apprenticed at an early age to the Parisian jeweller Edouard Marchand and later worked for the goldsmith and jeweller Dutreih. In 1847 he set up his own work-

shop at 2 Rue Favart and in the 1850s attained success with his naturalistic jewellery. By the early 1860s he was sufficiently well established to concentrate on antique themes. His interest in antique jewellery was stimulated, as for many other jewellers of the time, by Napoleon III's acquisition in 1861 of the Campana collection, consisting in part of antique jewellery, which came to the Louvre through the agency of Alessandro Castellani. Fontenay avoided servile imitation and produced highly artistic jewels set with pearls, lapis lazuli, coral and other gemstones which combined well with the matt richly coloured gold he used. Fontenay was interested in the art of enamelling, and in collaboration with Eugène Richet, a painter and miniaturist, he created a series of jewels mounted with opaque enamel plaques reminiscent of Pompeian frescoes decorated with figures taken from Greek mythology. Among his most successful jewels are those with amphora-shaped pendants, first created in 1865, and with pendants in the shape of oat or wheat grains first presented in 1867. The technical perfection and the beauty of the archaeological jewels he exhibited at the Exposition Universelle in Paris in 1867 won him a medal; their success confirmed the popularity of his style.

Between 1860 and 1867 Fontenay frequently worked for the East and Far East, producing jewels for the king of Siam, the Shah of Persia, the Indian market and the viceroy of Egypt. As a consequence of the French expedition in China and the conquest of Peking and the Summer Palace in 1860, a large number of imperial jades came to Paris, and Fontenay, fascinated by the Orient and by the beauty of the material, mounted them successfully in archaeologically inspired jewels. After a very distinguished career, he retired from business in 1882 to write a book, *Les Bijoux Anciens et Moderns* which was published in 1887.

Froment Meurice, François-Désiré (1802–1855)

A Parisian goldsmith and jeweller who took over the family business started by his father François Froment in 1792, and added to his surname that of Pierre Meurice, another goldsmith whom his mother remarried. Well trained in goldsmith's techniques and in the arts, he was very interested in sculpture and close to the artistic circles of his time. He became famous in the 1830s and 1840s for his romantically inspired jewels in Gothic revival and Renaissance style, which combined backgrounds of Gothic architecture with three-dimensional figures of knights, angels and saints cast in the round and decorated with polychrome enamels. Meurice triumphed in London at the Universal Exhibition of 1851 with his production in neo-Gothic and neo-Renaissance taste. His business was inherited by his son Emile.

Gérard, M.

The firm M. Gérard was founded in Paris in 1968 by Louis Gérard (Paris 1923) formerly of Van Cleef & Arpels. The new shop was opened in Avenue Montaigne and soon became renowned for jewels set with very high quality diamonds, mostly specimen stones. Business rapidly flourished, with outlets in Geneva, Lausanne, Gstaad, London, Monte Carlo, Cannes, New York; and by 1975 M. Gérard was announced to be the largest exporter of fine jewellery from France, a remarkable achievement against the well established French jewellers from across the Champs Elysées.

In 1985 a group of American investors bought the firm, Louis Gérard retired and a few years later the firm closed its door. At the end of 1987 it was reopened by its original owner at 16 Avenue Montaigne under the name Louis Gérard. Besides the exceptional quality of their diamonds and coloured stones, Gérard's jewels are always characterized by great suppleness and flexibility. The latter is achieved by technically very advanced mounts in which the weight of the metal is kept to a minimum and the number of solders and claws reduced. The resulting jewels are very supple and follow the contours of the female body which they adorn.

M. Gérard jewels are mainly signed: M. Gérard; or more recently: Louis Gérard.

Giuliano

A family of Neapolitan origin who became famous in London for their jewellery in Gothic and Renaissance style. The business was started by Carlo Giuliano (c.1831–1895), who was trained in Rome, possibly in the workshop of the Castellanis, where he produced jewels in the archaeological style. In about 1860 he moved to London and opened a workshop in Soho, in Frith Street, where he worked for various famous jewellers of the time such as Hunt & Roskell, C.F. Hancock and Robert Phillips. His jewels proved to be a success and in 1874 he opened his own shop at 115 Piccadilly.

Particularly attracted by the Renaissance, Giuliano studied the art of the Cinquecento and produced attractive jewels in neo-Renaissance style. He soon became famous for his pierced jewels delicately enamelled and set with pearls and precious or semiprecious gemstones. He eliminated colour almost completely from his compositions, covering the surface of the jewel with white and blue or black *piqué* enamel (*piqué* enamel consisting in decorating an enamelled surface with minute dots of enamel of contrasting colour). To the bright sparkle of facetted stones he always preferred the most discreet effect of cabochon gemstones. As the fashion for jewels in Renaissance style diminished, he relied less on that period as a source of inspiration, but his jewels never lost a certain Renaissance feel.

When he died the Piccadilly shop passed to his two sons: Carlo Joseph (dates unknown) and Arthur (c.1864–1914) who traded there until they moved to Knightsbridge in 1912. The Knightsbridge shop closed at the outbreak of the First World War. Carlo Joseph and Arthur Giuliano worked very much in the style of their father, possibly with a new interest in more delicate, pastel colour and flowery forms in line with the general trend of fashion.

The Giulianos always marked their pieces. The earliest pieces by Carlo Giuliano, in archaeological revival style, were often marked with a monogram CG very similar to the entwined Cs of Castellani. From 1863, Giuliano jewels were almost always signed with a monogram CG in an oval motif. After the death of their father, in 1896, Carlo Joseph and Arthur Giuliano entered a new mark consisting of the monogram C&AG in an oval motif.

Graff, Laurence

Laurence Graff has established the reputation of being one of the world's foremost producers of jewels set with rare and exceptional gems. His first outstanding sign of success came in 1973 when he became the first jeweller to be presented with the Queen's Award to Industry, an award which was repeated for further achievements in 1977. His shop at 55 Brompton Road, Knightsbridge, London is a place of pilgrimage for an élite clientèle in search of unique and magnificent gems. Graff is especially known for his diamonds and lately for coloured diamonds, a category which covers an entire spectrum from yellows, oranges, greens, blues – light to intense violet – to deep pink and red recently mined in Western Australia. Graff's designs are essential and his settings never overshadow the inherent beauty of the gems. Laurence Graff has set a nearly unsurpassable standard of excellence in his quest for 'perfect' gemstones and it has been said that more important gem quality diamonds have passed through his hands than through those of any other living dealer.

The firm's jewels are usually signed: Graff.

Grima, Andrew

Andrew Grima was born in Rome in 1921. He was educated in London and studied mechanical engineering at Nottingham University. In 1939 his studies were interrupted by the war and he served as an engineer in the army, mainly in India and Burma for five years. Undoubtedly he would have continued this career had he not married in 1946 the daughter of a Viennese jeweller who ran the firm of H. J. Co. Ltd. in London's Hatton Garden. In 1947 he left the army and engineering and joined his father's-in-law firm. In 1951, on the death of his father-in-law, he became chairman and managing director of H. J. Co.; in the following years business began to thrive again after the bleak post war period. By 1956 he was successfully designing and selling modern jewels. The break-through came in 1961, when his company won more prizes than any other in the De Beer Diamonds International Awards. In 1966 he won the Duke of Edinburgh Prize for Elegant Design, then the Queen's Award to Industry and Royal Warrant. In 1970 he was commissioned by Omega to design a prestige watch collection 'About Time' which was exhibited throughout the world. In 1965 he founded Andrew Grima Ltd and the opening of his striking slate-fronted shop in Jermyn Street followed in 1966; then New York and Sydney in 1970, Zurich in 1971 and three shops in Tokyo in 1973 and Lugano in 1987. Grima may be regarded as one of the most innovative designers of his time and the initiator of the movement of modern jewellery design in England. In defiance of conventional styles of jewellery Grima uses crystals in their natural forms, crystallized agates, opals, unusual shells and pearls characteristically set in rich textured gold with the emphasis on the design rather than on the intrinsic value of the materials. Since 1985 Andrew Grima has lived in Lugano with his wife Jojo and his daughter Francesca.

Andrew Grima's jewels are usually signed GRIMA in block capitals.

Hunt & Roskell

A London retail jewellery and goldsmith's shop of great fame and reputation who in 1846 succeeded Paul Storr's firm of Storr and Mortimer. They exhibited in the London Great Exhibition of 1851 and were renowned for their high quality products often in revivalist styles. They also acted as a retail outlet for Carlo Giuliano before he opened his own shop at 115 Piccadilly in 1874.

King, Arthur

Arthur King, born in New York in 1921, taught himself goldsmithing in the United States Navy during the war, when his duties as an overseer of an empty and unused troopship made him yearn to do something useful with his hands. Back in New York, King turned his attention fully to his new craft, gaining considerable recognition. His jewels are all one-offs and no two pieces, even a pair of earrings, are alike. The most remarkable aspects in his work are colour, unconventional materials and texture. Colourful and exotic organic materials – Biwa pearls from Japan, black Tahitian pearls, tortoiseshell from the Bahamas, fossilized prehistoric Jurassic shark's tooth, whales' and pigmy hippopotamus' teeth, ox-blood coral, Brazilian tourmalines, star sapphires from Burma and lavender jade from India – all find a place in his jewels, usually enveloped in rich gold settings. The latter are very organic in appearance, reminiscent of tendrils and sprawling roots, cast by means of the *cire perdu* method and frequently left unpolished and textured.

King won numerous awards and prizes for his jewellery design, including those of the Museum of Contemporary Crafts New York and the Cultured Pearl Association of Japan, and he was commissioned to design and create trophies utilizing native American materials for the National Trust for Historic Preservation Awards. His works have been extensively exhibited: in the Victoria and Albert Museum and the Goldsmiths' Hall International Jewellery Exhibition in London; Stockholm Museum of Modern Art, and the Museum of Natural Science in New York. He designed the jewels worn by Elizabeth Taylor in the film *Cleopatra*.

Arthur King has had some eighteen shops and outlets in Europe and America, but his headquarters have since 1970 been at 619 Madison Avenue, where he created an 'organic' decor in lead and steel to complement his 'organic' jewels. After his death in 1986 Arthur King's widow Louise took over the running of the business. King's jewels are usually signed either with the firm's name in capitals or with Arthur King's signature.

Kutchinsky

Kutchinsky began in 1893 when Polish immigrants settled in the East End of London and continued their profession by opening a small jewellery and watch repair shop. The business prospered and in 1913 Kutchinsky moved to larger premises at 171 Commercial Road, still in the East End.

Joe Kutchinsky, who was to become the major figure in the company's success, joined the family business in 1928 at the age of 14. He rapidly acquired skills in every area of the business, managing the firm to continuing success in the years leading up to the Second World War. During the war the shop partly closed down, but from 1945, Joe Kutchinsky forged ahead with a new commitment to design and technology and by the early 50s the firm had become well established in the world of fashion and jewellery. In 1958 it moved to the West End, taking up its current premises at 73 Brompton Road. Since this time Kutchinsky has developed royal patronage from several monarchies and an international reputation and continues to do so under the current Director Paul Kutchinsky who joined the company in 1971. After the war Kutchinsky began to pioneer new techniques which allowed them to create unique modern jewels. Among these innovations Kutchinsky developed a new successful gold, silver and platinum alloy for the manufacture of jewellery.

Most of Kutchinsky's jewels are inscribed with the signature Kutchinsky.

Lalaounis, Ilias

Ilias Lalaounis was born in Athens in 1920, the fourth generation of a family of goldsmiths originating from Delphi. After graduating in economics, he joined the family tradition and actively contributed to the revival of the art of Greek goldsmiths and jewellers. Firmly convinced that ancient pieces of jewellery, being works of art, could prove attractive to modern taste, he dedicated himself to the careful study of antique jewellery. In 1957 he exhibited at the Thessaloniki International Fair, his first collection of reproductions of ancient Greek pieces. The exhibition had a favourable response and from mere reproductions he moved to the creation of completely new lines of jewellery and objets d'art, being inspired by specific periods of ancient art. Sources of inspiration were offered to him not only by antique jewellery, but also by architectural or sculptural details, frescoes, mosaics, icons and even embroidery which were particularly characteristic of a certain era. As time passed, his horizon expanded from ancient and Byzantine Greece to Persia, the Arab world and the Jewish tradition, Japan, China, and lately to the arts of the Indians of North America. Nature, science and technology also offered Lalaounis inexhaustible sources of inspiration.

Ilias Lalaounis strongly believes that jewellery is a fine art, as long as its creator is able to communicate his feelings and his artistic impulse through his product, and stimulate emotions similar to those that art can evoke. At the same time he believes that the jeweller must be a man of his time, in touch with current trends, fashion and lifestyle because jewels have to be worn, and he is profoundly convinced that every piece of jewellery which is worthy of its name 'has a story to tell', it carries a message, is a link with the past, and is a symbol or a memory. His philosophy concerning the nature and function of jewellery is analyzed in his book *Metamorphoses* published in 1984, where his jewellery collections are pictured and discussed.

Ilias Lalaounis always favoured 22ct gold for his creations because of its warm colour, and he often uses carved and precious or semiprecious stones and diamonds to enhance his goldsmith's creations.

The Ilias Lalaounis Gallery and workshop based at the foot of the Acropolis in Athens, first opened in 1968, and was soon followed by the opening of sister galleries in Paris (1976), New York (1979), Hong Kong (1981) and London (1985). Ilias Lalaounis has been lately joined in his business by his four daughters Katerina, Dimitra, Maria and Ioanna. In February 1990 he was elected a full member of the Académie Française, the first creator in the field of the visual arts to receive this honour.

Ilias' jewels are signed with the full name in block capitals or stamped with his characteristic monogram in an egg-shaped motif.

Lalique, René (1860–1945)

René Lalique was the undisputed genius of Art Nouveau jewellery, a man of great talent and versatility who succeeded in transforming jewels from mere form of ornaments into great works of art. He was born at Ay, on the Marne, and since boyhood showed a deep interest in drawing and designing and in the study of nature. When his father died in 1876, he was forced to leave school and was apprenticed to the Parisian jeweller Louis Aucoq. After two years he moved to London to study at Sydenham College in South London, at a time when art schools there were known to be more progressive than in France. Back in Paris he worked as a freelance designer for various famous manufacturers such as Vever, Cartier and Boucheron. His designs of the 1880s conformed to the requirements of his clientèle, and were basically traditional, mainly set with diamonds. In 1885 he became independent but it was not until 1895 that he first publicly exhibited his jewels under his own name at the Salon de la Société des Artistes Français, where he obtained a remarkable success.

From the mid 1890s Lalique's jewellery begins to show a very strong sculptural element combined with the fluid and sinuous lines of Art Nouveau. Using gold with gemstones and enamel, he depicted motifs from nature, concentrating on fantasized insects such as dragonflies and butterflies and unusual flowers and plants. He focussed also on the decay and rebirth of the natural world by choosing dead flowers about to disintegrate in the wind and buds and blossoms. Another recurring motif in his jewellery is the female figure, nude or draped, twisted in the fluid lines of Art Nouveau and wrapped in flowing long hair. Lalique excelled in the art of *plique-à-jour* enamel, and from the late 1890s he began to incorporate moulded glass motifs in his creations. In the mid 1890s he began working for Sarah Bernhardt, the great tragic actress, and for many years he designed her large, flamboyant and melodramatic stage jewellery. His greatest success came after the Paris Exposition Universelle in 1900, where his jewels were very much admired and gained him many commissions from around the world. After 1910, disillusioned by the large number of bad quality imitations that his jewels had prompted, he devoted himself entirely to glassmaking.

His jewels are mainly signed either René Lalique or simply LALIQUE in block capitals.

Marina B

Marina Bulgari was born in Rome in 1930, the daughter of the renowned jeweller Costantino Bulgari. From an early age she began learning from her father all the intricacies and secrets of the art of jewellery making. After his death in 1973 she continued working in the family business until she broke away in 1979, setting up her own firm in Geneva under the name Marina B. Ever increasing success and international reputation has led her to open a shop in Monte Carlo and in 1986 another in Madison Avenue New York, designed by Gae Aulenti, and Milan in 1989. Among her distinctive pieces are: chokers sprung to fit perfectly the contours of the neck; reversible earrings, where a minute hinge mechanism allows a day earring to be converted into a dazzling evening piece; and a novel cut for gemstones known as the Marina B cut, which consists of a heart-shaped stone without the indentation. All Marina B's jewels are characterized by bold modern lines, by a great sense of volume and colour where precious and semiprecious stones are magnificently combined. Her pieces are commonly signed: Marina B., or with her initials MB.

Massin, Oscar (born 1829, retired from business 1892)

After an apprenticeship in Liège, Oscar Massin moved to Paris in 1851 where he worked for three years for Fester, using the rounded and spiky shapes of flowers and leaves. In 1854 he moved to Rouvenat and soon after to Viette, where he made the diadem worn by the Empress Eugénie at the opening of the Exposition Universelle of 1855. After eighteen months in London studying English jewellery, he returned to Paris where he joined Tottis and developed a more naturalistic and botanically accurate style; his floral compositions have great lightness and perfection. In 1863, refusing attractive proposals to work in London and in New York for Tiffany, he opened his own workshop in Paris. His designs of the 1860s are characterized by realistic leaves and flowers combined with ribbon bows, feathers, ears of wheat and rainfalls of diamonds. Between 1865 and 1870 he produced large, long pendent earrings with articulated cascades of diamonds on very light mounts that moved and reflected light at each movement of the head. Around 1865 he perfected his mounts, reducing to the minimum any intrusion of the setting metal and thus becoming a pioneer of the *monture illusion*. He also perfected the techniques of *pampille* and *tremblant* decoration, imitated by jewellers throughout Europe until the end of the century. His success at the 1867 Exhibition was enormous and he retained his leading position until he retired in 1892. For his superb workmanship, his sure taste and his innovations, he can be considered the principal reformer of 19th-century jewellery.

Mauboussin

Mauboussin was founded in 1827 by Mr Rocher and his cousin Baptist Noury. In 1850 Noury succeeded him and in 1876 took into partnership his nephew George Mauboussin. The latter in turn succeeded him in 1896, taking on as partner his cousin Marcel Goulet Mauboussin. The escalating success of the firm prompted the two cousins to move from the original site at 64 Rue Beaurepaire (the present Rue Grenta) to larger premises at 3 Rue de Choissell where it occupied an entire building with showroom, offices and workshop. Since the early 1920s George Mauboussin has been aware of the importance of increasing foreign exports and Mauboussin began opening branches and exhibiting internationally, from Rio de Janeiro to Athens, from Buenos Aires to New York. In 1924 George Mauboussin was awarded the Légion d'Honneur for his worldwide renown; in 1925 the firm won the Grand Prix at the famous Exposition Universelle des Arts Décoratifs, and thereafter continued to win prestigious awards at international exhibitions. It also organized special exhibitions, the 'Emerald', the 'Ruby' and the 'Diamond' of 1931, in which the firm displayed a unique diamond necklace set with 35 spherical diamond beads connected by diamond baguettes. It was patronized by an outstanding international clientèle including the Maharaja of Indore and Queen Nazli of Egypt, for whom Mauboussin reset all her jewels. After the Liberation in 1945 the firm moved to its present site at 20 Place Vendôme, the centre for French *haute joaillerie*. Here besides a jewellery showroom Mauboussin opened in 1955 a boutique where jewels of high quality but lower value are exhibited. At present Mauboussin has branches all over the world including four outlets in Japan and continues to thrive under Alain and Patrick Mauboussin. Most jewels are signed: MAUBOUSSIN in block capitals.

Meister

Meister was founded in October 1881 by Emil Meister in a small shop in the old town of Zurich. Success soon allowed him to move to a larger shop in the renowned Hotel Baur en Ville at the Paradeplatz. In 1941 Walter Meister took over the company from his father and brought it to international fame for the high quality of its gemstones, design and workmanship. In 1975 Meister moved their premises to a new and larger shop in the Bahnhof Strasse, but the silver division remained in the Baur en Ville. After the death of Walter Meister in 1986 the management of the company was taken over by his son Adrian Meister. Jewels by Meister are usually signed: E. Meister or EM.

Mellerio dits Meller

As far back as the 16th century the Mellerios were a Lombard family of jewellers. Following the battle of Marignano in 1515 they emigrated with numerous other northern Italians to Paris. Here they settled in the district of St-Merri. Among the arrivals were merchants, but also humble chimney-sweeps. According to a legend it was a young chimney-sweep from the town of Villette in Italy who discovered a plot against the young King Louis XIII and Marie de Médicis the regent, and it was revealed to the queen by the consul of the Lombards, Jean-Marie Mellerio. As a result of his service to the court, he and other Lombard craftsmen and workers were given royal protection under Marie de Médicis and the Mellerios in particular were distinguished by being called Mellerio dits Meller. The protection was renewed at various times especially when Italian artisans, such as jewellers and goldsmiths, suffered the unfair competition from Parisian and Provincial guilds. The 'King Registers' of the Parliament include documentation that the Mellerio family of jewellers and goldsmiths received full freedom to carry on their trade under Louis XIII in 1613 and in 1635, and again under Louis XIV in 1645, as well as in the time of Louis XV in 1716, 1760 and 1766. Thus Mellerio enjoyed the benefits of continued Royal patronage and protection. The family opened a shop in Rue des Lombards in 1750 and then in Rue Vivienne. During this time they worked for the court at Versailles and were patronized by Queen Marie Antoinette. During the revolution Jean-Baptiste Mellerio fled to Italy but returned to Rue Vivienne in 1796. Under the guidance of François Mellerio the epoque of the First Empire was one of great growth, as documented in the firm's record books, which survive from 1780 onwards. Among the famous names listed in these volumes are: Napoleon I and Empress Joséphine de Beauharnais, his sister Pauline Borghese and Caroline Murat, Queen of Naples, along with Marshals of the Empire and crown princes. At the time of the restoration Mellerio moved to 9 Rue de la Paix, the firm's present premises. During the July Monarchy (1830–1848) the house of Mellerio was jeweller to the Queen Amélie and Louis Philippe.

In 1848 Mellerio opened branches in Baden-Baden, in Madrid (1848), and in Biarritz (1862), where the Empress Eugénie and Napoleon III spent their summers and were among their best customers during the Second Empire (1852–1870). During these years numerous members of European royal families patronized Mellerio, including the queens of Belgium, Sweden and Great Britain. The archival collection of drawings that survive at Mellerio constitutes a unique testimony of the style of this period. It was also in the 19th century that Mellerio workshops became specialized in goldsmith's work for ecclesiastical purposes. Since 1936 Mellerio has also been creating Academicians' Swords and in the field of sports trophies such as the cup of the Roland Garros Tennis Tournament.

Mellerio dits Meller is today managed by the fourteenth generation of the family. François Mellerio is the president and Olivier Mellerio the managing director. Mellerio is also a member of La Haute Joaillerie de France and is the oldest company of the Comité Colbert which brings together the seventy prestigious firms of the luxury trade in France. Recently several shops have been opened in Japan where business is especially successful.

Mellerio jewels are usually signed in full: Mellerio dits Meller.

Nitot, Etienne (1750–1809)

After a humble start as a jeweller and watchmaker in a small workshop, Nitot became one of the most important French jewellers of the First Empire. Together with Foncier, another celebrated Parisian jeweller, he was commissioned to remount the jewels of the French crown on the occasion of the coronation of Napoleon in 1804. After Foncier's retirement, Nitot became the favoured jeweller of the Empress Joséphine. When he died in 1809, his firm passed to one of his four sons, François-Regnault Nitot, who was already his associate and continued to be the favourite jeweller of Napoleon and Joséphine. After 1815 François-Regnault Nitot retired, and his business was taken over by Fossin.

Peretti, Elsa

Elsa Peretti was born in Florence in 1940 and was educated in Rome. After receiving a degree in Interior Design, she worked for a Milanese architect. Later she went to New York and began modelling clothes for her designer friends. In 1969 she designed her first pieces of silver jewellery; a heart-shaped belt buckle and pendants shaped as small vases which were shown with Halston's collection. From then on she continued designing jewellery and in 1971 she received the Coty award for her jewellery designs. In 1974 Elsa Peretti joined Tiffany & Co and one of her first designs for the firm, 'Diamonds-By-The-Yard', created a sensation. In 1981 she received the Rhode Island School of Design President's Fellow Award, the College Albert Einstein Spirit of Achievement Award in 1983, and Fashion Group Night of the Stars Award in 1986. The Museum of Fine Arts, Boston, and the Museum of Fine Arts, Houston, host as part of their permanent collection objects by Elsa Peretti which have been donated by Tiffany & Co.

Elsa Peretti currently lives part of the year in Tuscany, Spain and New York and continues to design exclusively for Tiffany. Her designs rendered mainly in silver and gold are bold, characterized by sculptural biomorphic forms (beans, teardrops, and hearts) where the play of light and shadow commonly associated with sculpture is largely exploited.

Elsa Peretti signs her jewels PERETTI in block capitals, preceded or followed by TIFFANY & CO.

Phillips, Robert (1810–1881)

Robert Phillips was one of the most prominent jewellers in London working in the revivalist style. His shop was located at 31 Cockspur Street. He took part in the Paris Exhibition in 1867 where his jewels set with coral imported from Southern Italy and those in archaeological revival style had a great success. Under the influence of Sir Austen Henry Layard's excavations at Nineveh, he was particularly drawn to Assyrian art. He also designed jewels in Scandinavian taste and often mounted antique engraved gems in his jewels. Robert Phillips died in 1881, and by 1885 the ownership of the firm had passed to Alfred Phillips of 23 Cockspur Street, who entered at Goldsmiths' Hall a mark AP. Alfred Phillips had joined his father and uncle in business in 1869: it is legitimate therefore to assume that this partnership accounts for the subsequent use of a mark consisting of two Ps set back to back. The company ceased to trade in 1902.

Picasso, Paloma

Paloma Picasso was born in Paris in 1949. Her father was Pablo Picasso and her mother Françoise Gilot. Paloma spent her childhood in the south of France, was educated in Paris and attended the University of Paris Nanterre. In 1969, after she completed her formal training in jewellery design and goldsmithing, Yves St Laurent presented a collection of her costume jewellery. In 1972-73 Paloma Picasso designed gold jewellery for Zolotas. In 1973, when her father died, she devoted much of her time to assembling the collection for the Musée Picasso, which opened in Paris in 1983. Later Paloma Picasso resumed her initial vocation of jewellery designer, and in 1980 presented a collection for Tiffany & Co. The Field Museum of Natural History in Chicago acquired for their permanent collection a bracelet by Picasso set with 408.63 carats of moonstones decorated with 'lightning bolt' motifs pavé-set with diamonds. In 1984 Paloma Picasso backed by L'Oreal launched her perfume. In 1988, she received the Moda award from the Hispanic Designers, Inc, for her excellence in design, and was honoured by the Fashion Group's 'Night of the Stars' in their annual salute, 'Women Who Have Made an Extraordinary Impact on our Industry'.

Paloma Picasso's jewels may be distinguished for their generous scale and colour; often unexpected juxtapositions are exploited as well as large highly polished surfaces of precious metals, and among her favourite motifs are her 'lightning bolts'. Currently she continues to design for Tiffany and spends her time between Paris and New York.

Paloma Picasso's jewels are signed either PICASSO in capitals or with her own signature followed by TIFFANY & CO.

Pierret, Ernesto (1824–70)

Ernesto Pierret, born and educated in Paris, moved to Rome in the mid 1840s. By 1857 he was settled in his shop at 31 Piazza Firenze. He subsequently moved to 36 Via dell'Umiltà and finally to 20 Piazza di Spagna. He worked in the archaeological revival style, though in a less derivative manner than Castellani. His jewels are always well finished and show a considerable mastery of all the goldsmith techniques. He frequently used fine quality mosaics, intaglios and ancient coins in his creations. He also mastered the art of enamelling. Pierret usually signed his pieces, either with his name in full or, less frequently, with an elaborate monogram EP within a shield. At some point his business was taken over by Luigi Pierret, presumably a son, who exhibited jewellery in the archaeological style at the Turin Exhibition in 1884. The name of the firm disappears from Roman directories and guidebooks in 1890.

Repossi

The firm of Repossi was founded in Turin in the 1920s by Costantino Repossi, who began his activity first as designer and manufacturer of jewels for other important Italian firms. Rapid success soon enabled him to open his own outlet so that he could sell directly to the public. Costantino's sons Paolo and Alberto followed their father's steps. Paolo became responsible for the cutting of the precious gemstones and Alberto for designing. Alberto travelled for three years in the Far East to learn about selecting and buying precious gemstones. On one of his trips he came across a Burmese Buddha which has since become the symbol of the firm's attachment to Oriental art and culture. On 1977 Alberto, with the support of his future wife Gio, opened the first shop outside Italy in the Hermitage Hotel of Monaco. Soon after the young couple opened other shops abroad: in 1979 a second outlet in Monaco at the Hôtel de Paris, in 1980 in Kuwait and later in Paris at 6 Place Vendôme – one of the most renowned locations in the world for *haute joaillerie*. Alberto Repossi's designs are simple, devoid of superfluous lines, where carefully selected stones are set in unique mounts.

Schlumberger, Jean (1907–1987)

Jean Schlumberger was born in 1907 in Mulhouse, a town in German controlled Alsace, from a family of established textile manufacturers. In spite of Jean's early artistic inclinations, his family denied him any form of artistic training. He made his first trip to the United States in 1929 to learn English and to work in a New Jersey silk factory which he disliked intensely. He returned to Europe and his family sent him to London to learn typing and to Berlin to try his hand at banking. Once again this proved unsuccessful and he went to Paris. Here he first started work in the perfume department of Lucien Lelong and after a short time joined Braun & Co. art book publishers where he designed posters and catalogues. During his time in Paris he began collecting in flea markets odd pieces of gilt Victoriana, glass beads, porcelain flowers which he then transformed into costume jewellery. He soon became known for these fantasy jewels and was flooded with requests. He decided to give up his job with the art publishers and devote all his time to his *bijoux de fantaisie* by setting up his workshop in Rue de la Boetie. He was soon noticed by the designer Elsa Schiaparelli, who had particularly admired a pair of Schlumberger earrings worn by Marina, Duchess of Kent, some time in 1936–37. They were probably porcelain flowers or golden flying fish with diamond fins. Schiaparelli immediately commissioned Schlumberger to design a collection of buttons; some took the form of Chinese pink starfish and other bizarre fashion accessories caused a sensation in Paris. His successful collaboration with Schiaparelli came to an end in 1939 when Schlumberger joined the army at the outbreak of the Second World War. After the German invasion of France he was evacuated from Dunkirk to England and then fled to America. Once in New York he began designing gowns for Chez Ninon. Though successful, his desire was to continue his line of fantasy jewels in precious materials, a trend that he had initiated already in Paris in 1939 when he had designed a gold cigarette lighter in the form of a fish. By chance in New York he bumped into an old friend from Paris, Nicholas

Bongard, who was a nephew of the designer Paul Poiret and had worked in the jewellery trade for his uncle René Boivin and for Lacloche. They decided to go into business together and they set up a workshop at 745 Fifth Avenue, but in 1941 they both joined the Free French Forces of General de Gaulle and left for the Middle East.

In 1946 Schlumberger and Bongard returned to New York and established themselves at 21 East 63rd Street and also opened a shop in Paris. Throughout the late 1940s and 1950s Schlumberger's well-known repertory of jewellery was formed, he created the famous angels, birds, flowers, starfish and sea horses in which he juxtaposed vivid enamels, precious and semiprecious stones. From 1956 to 1976 he embarked upon a series of jewelled boxes and objects in the shape of cucumbers or melons, birds or palm trees in gold and enamel.

In 1956 Schlumberger and Bongard took up an offer of Tiffany's Chairman Walter Hoving whereby they set up an exclusive Schlumberger department on the mezzanine floor at Tiffany. Schlumberger retained complete control of his designs and his independent workshop in Paris and at the same time became vice president of Tiffany & Co. In 1958 Schlumberger was the first jeweller to receive the Fashion Critics Award and in 1961 a retrospective exhibition of 85 Schlumberger pieces was held in the Manhattan's Wildenstein Gallery. In 1978 Schlumberger closed his Paris workshop and in the early 1980s left New York and his Caribbean home to retire in Paris where he died in 1987. Today the Schlumberger department at Tiffany continues to thrive under the supervision of Nicholas Bongard and Stephen Collins.

The jewels designed by Jean Schlumberger for Tiffany & Co are signed SCHLUM-BERGER in block capitals, followed or preceded by TIFFANY & CO.

Serafini, Enrico (1913–68)

Enrico Serafini was born in Florence in 1913, and as an apprentice goldsmith worked on souvenirs of Florence, such as reproductions of Donatello sculptures in bronze. He taught himself to design jewellery, and in 1947, after selling his designs to others, he set up his own workshop at 4 Piazza Santa Felicità. Here he thrived and soon became well known in Florence and abroad, especially in North America. During the 1950s he created very imaginative jewels using designs based on unusual flowers or vegetables and exotic animals. His work is always characterized by a great sculptural quality, by bright polychrome enamels set with gemstones or carved hardstones. In 1957 he was the first Italian to win the Diamonds International Award, which gained him further international reputation. Among his clients were Adlai Stevenson, Mrs Stavros Niarchos, Countess Consuelo Crespi, Princess Irene Galitzine, and Marquis Emilio Pucci. In the second decade of his activity his designs become more abstract, characterized by an interest in the texture of gold and reflecting the 1960s trend of jewellery design. Serafini was a sensitive artist who responded to the artistic movements of his day but was always able to reinterpret them in a personal idiom. He died in January 1968. Serafini's jewels are usually signed: E. Serafini.

Sterlé, Pierre

Pierre Sterlé was born into a family of high ranking financial officials. At the death of his father during the First World War, he was cared for by an uncle who was a jeweller in the Rue de Castiglione. This initial exposure to the world of jewellery was to prove of paramount importance for the choice of Pierre's subsequent career. After having worked for various jewellers Sterlé opened his own business in 1934 on the sixth-floor in premises in Rue Saint

Anne. Subsequently he moved to the Rue des Moulins and then in 1945 to the third-floor of 43 Rue de l'Opéra refusing to exhibit his work in a ground-floor shop window. The firm closed its doors in the early 60s. Sterlé's work is appreciated for its originality and for the fact that it epitomizes the spirit of the 40s and 50s. His jewels are usually signed: Sterlé Paris.

Tiffany & Co.

The firm Tiffany & Young was founded by Charles Lewis Tiffany (New England in 1812–New York 1902) with his partner John B. Young with premises at 259 Broadway, New York. The firm began by selling novelties and stationery, later adding French, German and English jewellery together with Bohemian crystals and Dresden porcelain. In 1841 the expanding business brought in another partner, J.L. Ellis, and the firm was then called Tiffany, Young & Ellis. Their increasing success in selling European jewellery led the firm to open a branch in Paris under the name Tiffany, Reed & Co. In 1848 Tiffany managed to purchase the famous diamond girdle of Marie Antoinette and in 1887 to buy 24 lots from the sale of the French crown jewels. By 1853 Young and Ellis retired from the partnership and the firm became simply Tiffany & Co. with new premises at 550 Broadway.

From 1851 the renowned American silversmith John C. Moore began designing exclusively for Tiffany. At the Paris Exhibition of 1878 Tiffany received the first place gold medal for silver craftsmanship and a gold medal for its jewellery. This was the first time an American company was so honoured by a foreign jury. In 1870 the famous six-pronged 'Tiffany Setting' for diamond solitaires was introduced and in 1877 the 'Tiffany Diamond', a fancy yellow diamond of 287 carats, was found and cut down to a stone weighing 128 carats.

Furthering the firm's dedication to and reputation for excellence in design, Louis Comfort Tiffany (1848–1933), the famed artist and son of Tiffany & Co.'s founder, became the firm's first Director of Design, a post he held from 1902 through 1918. During that time, an entire floor of Tiffany & Co. was devoted to merchandise crafted in Tiffany Studios – Louis Comfort Tiffany's atelier – as well as to colourful jewellery.

Nowadays Tiffany & Co. continues in its tradition of supporting quality and excellence of design. At present Tiffany & Co. has one of the largest collections of fine jewellery with its special collections created exclusively for Tiffany by Jean Schlumberger, Elsa Peretti and Paloma Picasso as well as silver, china, crystal, timepieces, stationery, leather accessories, scarves and fragrance. In addition to its landmark store located at Fifth Avenue and 57th Street in New York, Tiffany operates eleven branches throughout the United States. Internationally Tiffany has shops in London, Munich, Hong Kong and Zurich and sells Tiffany products through Faraone shops in Milan and Florence, and through Mitsukoshi in Japan and Hawaii.

Tiffany & Co. jewels are usually signed: Tiffany & Co.

Trabert & Hoffer Inc. – Mauboussin

The American firm of Trabert & Hoffer, Inc. was located at 522 Fifth Avenue in the Guaranty Trust Building. It also had a branch in Paris at 58 Rue Lafayette and one in Detroit, Michigan at 120 Madison Avenue. Its association with Mauboussin of Paris began in 1929, when Mauboussin decided to open a branch in New York. The new Mauboussin outlet was inaugurated on the 1st of October just a few weeks before the Wall Street Crash. The Parisian firm was then left with a large stock in the United States and in an attempt to withdraw with minimum losses, Mauboussin reached an agreement with Trabert & Hoffer,

Inc. whereby they would take on Mauboussin's stock and name. The new business was called Trabert & Hoffer, Inc. – Mauboussin.

By the early 30s, Trabert & Hoffer, Inc. – Mauboussin moved premises to Park Avenue and 57th Street and expanded, creating branches in Los Angeles, Atlantic City, Miami Beach, Palm Beach and Paris.

The firm was best known for a line of jewels called 'Reflection – Your Personality in a Jewel'. Reflection jewels were mainly in yellow 18 carat gold set with semiprecious stones. Made up of relatively cheap cast elements, they could be assembled in different combinations according to the customer's personal taste and style. After the war in 1946 Trabert & Hoffer, Inc. broke their connection with Mauboussin.

Their jewels are normally signed: Trabert & Hoffer
MAUBOUSSIN.

Van Cleef & Arpels

Offspring of diamond dealers for several generations, Alfred Van Cleef (1873–1938) and his two brothers-in-law Charles Arpels (1880–1951) and Julien Arpels (1884–1964) founded a jewellery firm in 1898 with small premises at 34 Rue Drouot. Later in 1912 the youngest Arpels brother Louis (1886–1976) joined the family business. Rapid success led them to move in 1906 to larger and more prestigious premises at 22 Place Vendôme, enlarged to their present size in 1932. From 1906 on the firm began opening branches in elegant holiday resorts, first in Dinard, then Nice, Deauville, Vichy, Cannes (1921), Monte Carlo (1935), and later overseas: New York in 1939 was to be the first of countless branches scattered all over the world. Van Cleef & Arpels also exhibited their jewels extensively in international exhibitions and received the Grand Prix at the Paris Exposition of 1925. From 1926 to 1942 Renée Puissant, daughter of Alfred Arpels, was appointed artistic director assisted by the designer René-Sim Lacaze, who was associated with the firm from 1922 until 1939. This team proved extremely successful and Van Cleef & Arpels were always at the forefront with their innovative and elegant designs. In 1930 Van Cleef & Arpels created the *Minaudière*, a jewelled evening bag fitted with numerous accessories, and in 1935 began producing jewels realized with the invisible setting technique.

Around 1935 the three sons of Julien Arpels: Claude (1911), Jacques (1914) and Pierre (1919–1980) began to be involved in the family business. The eldest took charge, in 1939, of the New York branch; while Jacques and Pierre remained in France, the first developing an expertise in precious stones, the second looking after the public relations of the firm. In 1954 Van Cleef & Arpels opened a *Boutique* department with the purpose of selling attractive jewels which would be more affordable and less exclusive but always of high quality.

The continuity of the family tradition has been ensured by the third and present generation: Philippe Arpels and Dominique Hourtoulle, son and daughter of Jacques Arpels, and Caroline Daumen, daughter of Pierre Arpels, who joined the business in the mid 70s. Philippe specializes in gemstones, Dominique contributes to the creation of the *Haute Joaillerie* and *Boutique* jewels as well as public relations, while Dominique is in charge of the publicity department.

Van Cleef & Arpels jewels are usually signed and bear a stock number. At times the signature is in full either in script or in block capitals, followed by the name or names of their branches, Paris and New York, or at times simply with the initials VCA. The firm's mark is illustrated on p. 147 of Raulet, S., *Van Cleef & Arpels*, Paris, 1986.

Verdura

Fulco Santostefano della Cerda, Duke of Verdura, was born in Sicily in 1898. Family debts and an extravagant masked ball held in Palermo forced Verdura, as he came to be known, to earn his own living. Fascinated by the wealth and beauty of Italian art, Verdura always had a desire to pursue a career as a painter, and in 1927 he moved to Paris where he began designing textiles for Coco Chanel. Under her influence he began designing jewellery as well. Among his designs for Chanel were earrings set with large pearls roped in gold and a pair of black-and-white enamel bracelets mounted with jewelled Maltese crosses. His success at Chanel prompted Verdura to try his luck in the United States, where he began working, in 1937, both in Hollywood and New York for the jeweller Paul Flato.

In 1939 he established his own firm in New York at 712 Fifth Avenue. Here his business prospered attracting a host of American and international patrons. His jewels always combine impeccable workmanship with the unexpected and the whimsical. Animals, flowers, shells and objects are brought to life in a countless variety of gems. As time passed Verdura's work came to have a great impact on other jewellers. His shell jewellery influenced Seaman Schepps and Margaret Stynx. His extensive use of bright and colourful enamels was a trend which was followed both by David Webb and Schlumberger. In 1973 Verdura sold his business to an associate before retiring to London. The business, now at 745 Fifth Avenue, was bought in 1985 by Edward Landrigan who with his wife Judith continues to offer Verdura's designs, favoured now as much as in the past.

Verdura jewels are commonly signed: VERDURA.

Webb, David

David Webb was born in 1925 and began working from the age of eleven in his uncle's workshop in Ashville, North Carolina. At the age of sixteen he left for New York where he was to complete his apprenticeship in various workshops. In 1946 he founded his firm in partnership with Nina Silberstein with premises on 47th Street. Then in the early 50s he moved to the first floor of 6 West 57th Street where he continues to sell his jewels mainly wholesale to Bergdorf Goodman and Bonwit Teller and only to a few private clients. In 1963 the showroom of David Webb Inc. was opened at 7 East 57th Street. Webb soon gained an international reputation for his unusual menagerie of enamelled frogs, tigers, lions and for jewels created with indigenous American materials or inspired by American themes and motifs.

The jewels are usually signed either David Webb or simply Webb.

Winston, Harry (1896–1978)

Harry Winston was born in New York City in 1896. He began his career in jewellery at the age of fifteen in Los Angeles. In his late teens he returned to New York and, using $2,000 he had saved while in California, set up a one-man firm, the Premier Diamond Company, in a small office on Fifth Avenue. Winston's success was based on finding fine gems beyond the conventional sources such as estate jewellery. At first he established strong working relationships with bankers in the area. Then using the Social Register and Who's Who, he proceeded to offer his services to the wealthy. By 1932, when he established Harry Winston Inc. at 718 Fifth Avenue, he had already been involved in numerous transactions that ran as high as a million dollars.

Over the years Harry Winston has held more than 60 of the world's 303 major diamonds

– more than any individual, including governments and royalty. The company has sold some of the world's largest diamonds including: the Jonker, Vargas, Star of Sierra Leone and the Taylor-Burton, and has donated to the Smithsonian Institution in Washington the notorious Hope diamond. Since 1949 the firm has initiated a tradition of private and public exhibitions of rare jewels. The 'Court of Jewels' exhibition which included diamonds such as the Hope, Star of the East, Indore Pear Shapes, Jonker, McLean and Mabel Boll, and an abundance of rubies, emeralds and sapphires, among them the enormous 337 carat Catherine the Great sapphire, made its debut at Rockefeller Center in 1949 and toured the United States until the mid 50s raising money for charitable purposes. Not since the British Crown Jewels were put on display had such an exhibition been made available to the public. In more recent years Harry Winston has held other exhibitions including: the 1982 display at the Metropolitan Museum of Art, New York to celebrate the firm's 50th Anniversary, and the 1985 exhibitions at Los Angeles Museum of Natural History and Field Museum of Natural History Chicago.

A unique feature among *hauts joailliers* is that Harry Winston has extensive wholesale and manufacturing operations in addition to retail salons in New York, Geneva, Paris, Monte Carlo, Beverly Hills and now in Tokyo. The specialized operation of cutting the rough diamond, polishing, designing and creating the finished jewel, is conducted in Winston's New York building on Fifth Avenue. Distinctive features of Winston jewels, besides the exceptional quality of the stones, are light settings where the precious metal is kept to a minimum and designs frequently consisting of cluster arrangements of marquise and pear-shaped stones.

Since the death of Harry Winston in 1978, the firm has been headed by his son Ronald who is building on the solid foundations of the Winston reputation in order to take the firm into fresh directions for a new era.

Harry Winston jewels are usually signed either in full: Harry Winston, or Winston.

Glossary

'a baule': (Italian) a type of Etruscan earring, the outline of which recalls a travelling case, hence the name. It consists of a decorated strip of gold bent to form an almost complete cylinder, fitted to the earlobe by means of gold wire.

aigrette: a gold or silver hair ornament to support a real feather or a jewel in the shape of a feather or spray of flowers. Often shaped as an egret plume (hence the name) it was usually set with many small gemstones. Aigrettes were in fashion from the 17th to the late 18th century and again in the late 19th and early 20th centuries.

baguette: a gemstone, usually a diamond, cut so that the table is in the shape of a long, narrow rectangle, bordered by four trapeze-shaped facets.

beading: a form of jewellery decoration by which the ornament is applied with small beads or globules of the same metal, usually gold.

brilliant-cut: the most common style of cutting a diamond. The standard brilliant-cut consists of 58 facets, 33 on the top or crown of the stone, and 25 on the base or pavilion. The crown has a large 8-sided central facet called the table. The culet is the small facet of the pavilion, parallel to the table. The girdle is the line where the pavilion and the crown meet. The original brilliant-cut is said to have been invented by the Italian Vincenzo Peruzzi about 1700, and quickly superseded the former rose-cut.

briolette: a diamond or other transparent gemstone pear-shaped drop cut in a style that is a modification of the rose-cut, having the entire surface cut in small triangular facets.

cabochon: a domed gemstone with a high polished curved surface but no facets. It is usually cut from an opaque or translucent stone although some rubies, emeralds, sapphires, amethysts and garnets have been cut in this style. There are four types of cabochons:
1) the simple cabochon with a domed top and a flat base.
2) The double cabochon with a domed top and a domed underside.
3) The hollow cabochon with a domed top and the interior cut away so as to obtain a shell-like form.
4) the tallow-topped or low domed cabochon with a very shallow dome.

calibré-cut: a style of cutting a gemstone, usually of small dimension, in a shape that will fit perfectly into the shape of the mount.

cannetille: a decoration of fine gold or silver wires twisted into the form of scroll and rosette motifs similar to filigree, often incorporating shells and burr-like motifs. It is named after a type of embroidery made with fine twisted gold or silver threads.

claw-setting: a style of setting of a gemstone by which the gem is held in place by a series of projecting prongs (claws). This type of setting was developed in the 19th century and is used mainly for transparent facetted gemstones as it allows light to enter the lower part of the stone therefore improving its fire and brilliancy.

collet-setting: a style of setting a stone by which the gem is fitted in a circular, square, hexagonal or otherwise shaped 'box' made from a thin metal band or 'collet'.

culet: the small facet at the base – or pavilion – of a brilliant-cut stone, parallel to the table.

embossing: a technique of producing a relief decoration by raising the surface of the metal from the reverse in the required pattern. This technique is the same as repoussé but the term is sometimes strictly applied to the work done mechanically by means of stone or metal dies.

faience: an imprecise but convenient term for a glazed siliceous mass where the body is a fused mass of ground or crushed quartz. Coloured faience is produced by adding to the original ground quartz the colouring agent which will migrate to the surface when fired to give a glaze, or by painting with a pigment solution the dried crushed quartz core which is subsequently fired.
Faience first occurs in Northern Mesopotamia possibly as early as the 5th millennium BC, and hence spread to Sumeria and Egypt where it was very popular in the form of beads used in jewellery from the 3rd millennium BC.

fibula: a type of ancient garment-fastener brooch usually consisting of a straight pin coiled at one end to form a spring and extended back to form a bow and a catch-plate to secure the pin.

filigree: a type of decoration on metalware made by use of fine gold or silver wire twisted or plaited into intricate but delicate patterns. In some cases the wire is applied to a metal base, in others it is worked into an openwork pattern, without a metal foundation.

girandole: a type of brooch or earring consisting, in its simplest form, of a cluster or single circular stone surmount supporting three pear-shaped drops. There are several variations of the base design where the surmount assumes more elaborate shapes of ribbon bows, sprays of leaves and flowers sometimes embellished with hearts, doves or trophies of love.

granulation: a gold-working technique in which minute spherical grains of gold are applied and invisibly soldered to a metal surface forming decorative patterns. The process of granulation was known to the goldsmiths of the Eastern Mediterranean from as early as the 3rd millennium BC, and was largely used by the Greeks and refined especially by the Etruscans. The technique was revived by the 19th-century jewellers working in the archaeological style.

intaglio: a technique of gem engraving where the gemstone is engraved below the level of its prepared flat and polished surface. The term intaglio is perhaps better understood if explained as the opposite of a cameo.

jarretière: literally, garter. A type of ornament, usually a bracelet but occasionally also a ring or an earring, resembling a strap with a buckle.

mabe pearl: a type of cultured pearl in the form of a blister pearl obtained by cementing a spherical bead of mother-of-pearl to the nacreous internal surface of an oyster shell and returning the oyster to the water where the bead is quickly covered by a coat of nacre. The bead is subsequently cut off the shell and its lower part, not covered by the nacreous substance, ground off and replaced with a piece of mother-of-pearl. The non-nacreous base is usually covered by a closed-back setting when mounted in jewellery.

marquise: a diamond or other transparent gemstone that is cut in a modification of the brilliant-cut, so that the girdle is boat-shaped.

millegrain-setting: a style of setting of a gemstone by which the stone is secured in the collet by a series of minute adjacent beads (grains) of metal which are raised by passing a knurling tool (millegrain tool) around the top edge of the collet.

Nike: in Greek mythology the goddess of victory (Greek νίϰη), the daughter of the Titan Pallas and of Styx, the Nymph of the homonymous Underworld subterranean river. In works of art she is represented as a female winged figure, often carrying a palm branch or a wreath; frequently hovering with outspread wings over the victor in a competition, since her functions referred not only to success in war, but to all other human undertakings. In fact Nike gradually came to be recognized as a sort of mediator to success between gods and men.

palmette: a fan-shaped or stylized foliate motif with units arranged symmetrically round a central stem, resembling a palm-leaf.

pampille, en: a style of decorating jewellery in the form of articulated cascades of gemstones graduated in size from the top and terminating with tapered pointed drops.

parure: a suite of matching jewellery usually comprising a necklace, a pair of earrings and a bracelet; brooches and hair ornament are often included.
Less than a full set is called a demi-parure.

pavé-setting: a style of setting gemstones by which many stones usually of small dimensions are set very close to each other so as to cover the entire surface almost conceal the metal.

pear-shaped: a style of cutting of a diamond or other transparent gemstone in a modification of the brilliant-cut, so that the girdle is pear-shaped.

pectoral: a decorative ornament worn on the breast.

pendeloque: a form of earring comprising a marquise-shaped, oval or circular surmount supporting a ribbon bow motif and an elongated drop, particularly fashionable in the second half of the 18th century.

repoussé: a technique of producing a relief decoration by means of raising the pattern from the reverse with a punch and hammer. The work is done manually but often the term is used to describe the similar mechanical process of embossing by means of stone or metal dies.

rose-cut: a style of cutting of a diamond or other transparent gemstone having a flat base and a pointed dome cut with triangular facets.

rose diamond: a diamond having its facets cut in the rose-cut style.

Sévigné: a type of brooch in the shape of a ribbon bow sometimes supporting small drops very popular in the 17th and 18th centuries. It was named after the Marquise de Sévigné (1626–1696), a member of the court of Louis XIV.

surmount: in a pendent earring the upper part of the jewel, worn in contact with the earlobe.

step-cut: a style of cutting a diamond or other gemstone so that below the rectangular, square, hexagonal or octagonal table there are a varying number of sloping parallel rows of four-sided facets which give the impression of steps.

swing centre: the central decorative motif of certain pendants and pendent earrings which is free to move and swing, being suspended within a similarly shaped frame.

Bibliography

ALDRED, C., *Jewels of the Pharaoh*, London, 1971.

BECKER, V., *Art Nouveau Jewellery*, London, 1985.

BECKER, V., *Antique and Twentieth Century Jewellery*, London, 1st ed. 1980, 2nd ed. 1987.

BECKER, V., *Fabulous Fakes*, London, 1988.

BENNETT, D., MASCETTI, D., *Understanding Jewellery*, Woodbridge, 1989.

BLACK, A., *Storia dei Gioielli*, Novara, 1973.

BRADFORD, E., *Four Centuries of European Jewellery*, London, 1953.

BURY, S., *Jewellery Gallery Summary Catalogue*, Victoria and Albert Museum, London, 1983.

CARTLIDGE, B., *Twentieth-Century Jewelry*, New York, 1985.

CARUSO, I., *Collezione Castellani: Le Oreficerie*, Roma, 1988.

CRISTOFANI, M., MARTELLI, M., *L'Oro degli Etruschi*, Novara, 1983.

CULME, J., RAYNER, N., *The Jewels of the Duchess of Windsor*, London, 1987.

DALLORO, G., 'Gemme Nummarie', *FMR*, n.71, 1989, p. 33 ff.

DE JONG, E., 'Pearls of virtue and pearls of vice', *Simiolus*, Vol. 8, 1975-1976, p.69 ff.

ELEUTERI, C., BELARDI, G., *Antichi Orecchini*, Roma.

EVANS, J., *A History of Jewellery 1100–1870*, London, 1st ed. 1953, 2nd ed. 1970.

FLOWER, M., *Victorian Jewellery*, London, 1951.

FONTENAY, E., *Les Bijoux Anciens et Modernes*, Paris, 1887.

FREGNAC, C., *Jewellery from the Renaissance to Art Nouveau*, London, 1965.

GABARDI, M., *Les Bijoux de l'Art Déco aux Années 40*, Paris, 1980.

GABARDI, M., *Gioielli Anni '50*, Milano, 1986.

GREGORIETTI, G., *Il Gioiello nei Secoli*, Milano, 1969.

GERE, C., *Victorian Jewellery Design*, London, 1982.

GERE, C., *European and American Jewellery*, London, 1985.

GERE, C., RUDOE, J., TAIT, H., WILSON, T., *The Art of the Jeweller, A Catalogue of the Hull Grundy Gift to the British Museum*, London, 1984.

GERE, C., MUNN, G., *Artists' Jewellery, Pre-Raphaelite to Arts and Crafts*, Woodbridge, 1989.

Gli Ori di Taranto in Età Ellenistica, Milano, 1984 (Exhibition Catalogue).

HACKENBROCH, Y., *Renaissance Jewellery*, Munich, 1979.

HIGGINS, R.A., *Greek and Roman Jewellery*, London, 1961.

HINKS, P., *Nineteenth Century Jewellery*, London, 1975.

HINKS, P., *Twentieth Century Jewellery 1900–1980*, London, 1983.

HOFFMANN, H., DAVIDSON, P., *Greek Gold*, Brooklyn, 1965.

JEDDING-GESTERLING, *Hairstyles*, Hamburg, 1988.

KELLEY, L., SHIFFER, N., *Costume Jewelry*, Pennsylvania, 1987.

KRASHES, L., *Harry Winston: The Ultimate Jeweler*, New York, 1st ed. 1984, 2nd ed. 1986, 3rd ed. 1988.

LALAOUNIS, I., *Metamorphoses*, 1984.

Les Fouquet, Bijoutiers & Joailliers à Paris, 1860–1960, Musée des Arts Décoratifs, Paris, 1983, (Exhibition Catalogue).

MASCETTI, D., *Gioielli dell'Ottocento*, Novara, 1984.

MASCETTI, D., *Oreficerie del Settecento*, Novara, 1985.

MEDVEDEVA, G., PLATONOVA, N., POSTNI-KOVA-LOSEVA, M., SMORODINOVA, G., TROEPOLSKAYA N., *Russian Jewellery 16th-20th Centuries from the Collection of the Historical Museum, Moscow*, Moscow, 1987.

MOREL, B., *The French Crown Jewels*, Antwerp, 1988.

MULVAGH, J., *Costume Jewellery in Vogue*, London, 1988.

MUNN, G., *Castellani and Giuliano, Revivalist Jewellers of the Nineteenth Century*, London, 1984.

NADELHOFFER, H., *Cartier: Jewellers Extraordinary*, London and New York, 1984.

NERET, G., *Boucheron Four Generations of a World-Renowned Jeweller*, Paris, 1988.

O'DAY, D., *Victorian Jewellery*, London, 1st ed. 1974, 2nd ed. 1982.

OGDEN, J., *Jewellery of the Ancient World*, London, 1982.

Ori e Argenti di Sicilia, Milano, 1989, (Exhibition Catalogue).

Princely Magnificence: Court Jewels of the Renaissance, London, 1980, (Exhibition Catalogue).

PRODDOW, P., HEALE, D., *American Jewelry, Glamour and Tradition*, New York, 1987.

RAULET, S., *Art Déco Jewelry*, Paris, 1984.

RAULET, S., *Van Cleef & Arpels*, Paris, 1986.

RYBAKOV, B.A., (ed.), *Treasures of the USSR Diamond Fund*, Moscow, 1980.

SNOWMAN, A.K., *Carl Fabergé*, London, 1980.

SCARISBRICK, D., *Jewellery*, London, 1984.

SCARISBRICK, D., *Ancestral Jewels*, London, 1989.

STEINBRABER, E., *Antique Jewellery, its History in Europe from 800 to 1900*, London, 1957.

VEVER, H., *La Bijouterie Française au XIXe Siècle*, Paris, 1908.

Acknowledgments

Our first thanks go to all our colleagues at Sotheby's in the Jewellery Departments in London, Geneva, New York, Milan and Paris for their help during our project. We are particularly grateful to David Bennett, Franca Galbiati, Hervé d'Oncieu and Nicholas Rayner for their encouragement and support. Invaluable help has been supplied by Felicity Nicholson, Antiquities Department; Tom Eden, Coins Department; Kerry Taylor, Collectors Department; Elena Mondelli, Old Master Paintings Department; Don Victor Franco de Baux, Silver Department; Haydn Williams, Vertue Department and the students on the Sotheby's Works of Art Course 1989–90 who helped us with the iconographic research.

We also would like to thank the following for the generously provided advice, suggestions, information and photographic material: Marcello Aldega, Rome; Marit Guinness Aschan, London; Vivienne Becker, London; Shirley Bury, London; Boucheron Paris: Michel Tonnelot, Pierre Robert; Bulgari London: Daniel Reveyron; Bulgari Rome: Catherine Robert; Cartier Geneva: Eric Nussbaum; Cartier London: Teresa Buxton; Cartier Paris: Betty Jais; Chaumet Paris: Beatrice De Plinvalle; Philippe Daudy, London; Robert Dobrick, London; James Colville, London; Eleuteri Rome: Carlo Eleuteri; Ralph Esmerian, New York; Carlo Ferrero, Rome; Gerda Flockinger, London; Elisabetta Franchi Corbella, Milan; Louis Gerard Paris: Louis Gerard; David Gol, Geneva; Graff London: Gwendoline Farrow; Laura Grandi, Milan; Andrew Grima, Lugano: Andrew Grima; Nicholas Harris, London; Debra Healy, New York; Lewis Kaplan Associates, London: Gordon Watson; Arthur King, New York: Louise King; Mrs Ian Krugier, Geneva; Kutchinsky, London: David O'Connor; Ilias Lalaounis Gallery, London: Ilias Lalaounis, Lily Wilkinson; Marina B, Geneva: Marina Bulgari, Yvonne Lucas; Maritiem Museum, Rotterdam: Leo Akveld; Mauboussin, Paris: Michel Robert; Meister, Zurich; Mellerio dits Meller, Paris: Nicole Meyrat; Arthur Millner, London; Martin Moody, London; Geoffrey Munn, London; Obsidian London: Harry Fane; Jack Ogden, London; Lilly and Ernesto Panier Bagat, Rome; S. J. Phillips, London: Jonathan Norton, Michael Bell; Repossi, Montecarlo; Diana Scarisbrick, London; Schlumberger Department, Tiffany & Co. New York: Stephen J. Collins; Rita Severis, Sotheby's Cyprus; Michael Snowdin, Print Department, Victoria and Albert Museum London; Tiffany & Co., New York: Marisa Radovich; Tiffany & Co, London: Lada Skrablin, Sibilla Tomacelli; Elena Travelli, Sotheby's, Geneva; Geoffrey Turk, London; Verdura, New York: Edward and Judith Landrigan, Jennifer Celata; Patrizia Verduchi, Faculty of Archaeology, Rome University; David Webb, New York: Stanley Silberstein; Harry Winston, New York: Laurence Krashes; Harry Winston, Paris: Marie Claude Parnaud.

Photographic Acknowledgements
We are grateful to Sotheby's Photographic
Departments in London, Geneva, New York and
Milan for their generosity in providing icon-
ographic material. We would like to thank in
particular Eddie Edwards, London; and Michael
Oldford, New York.
Our thanks go also to the following photogra-
phers:
Otello Bellamio, Milan; Lucinda Douglas-Men-
zies, London; Ingrid Hammond, Rome; Alain
Notz, Geneva; Saulmes, Paris; Seberger, Paris;
John Speakes, London.
Unless otherwise credited, all photographs are
courtesy of Sotheby's.

Museums and galleries
Cyprus Museum: 25 (except right hand
   column), 32, 33 (top)
Ferrara Archaeological Museum, photo Istituto
   Geografico de Navara/G. Nimotallah: 30
   (bottom)
Florence, Uffizi: 36 (top left)
Lavinium Antiquarium: 30–31 (top)
London, British Museum: 26–27 (top), 31 (top
   right) (photo Istituto Geografico de Agostini,
   Navara), 33 (bottom), 40 (top), 102–103
   – Victoria and Albert Museum: 38–39 (except
   portrait), 57, 79 (top right)
   – Worshipful Company of Goldsmiths: 177
   (top left)
Rome, Villa Giulia, photos Istituto Geografico de
   Agostini, Navara/G. Nimotallah: 28 (bot-
   tom), 29 (bottom left and right), 34 (right)
Tarentum, National Archaeological Museum,
   photos Arnoldo Mondadori Arte Milane, by
   Araldo De Luce, Rome: 25 (right hand
   column), 26–27 (except top), 31 (bottom
   right), 35 (bottom)
Vatican, Museo Gregoriano Etrusco, photos Istituto Geografico de Agostini, Navara/G.
   Nimotallah: 30 (bottom left), 35 (top)
Volterra, Museo Guarnacci, photo Istituto Geografico de Agostini, Navara/G. Nimotallah:
   34 (left)

Designers and archives
Aldega, Marcello (Rome): 90 (portrait)
Boucheron Archives (Paris): 155 (right), 165
(Bijoux poster), 170 (left and bottom), 171,
   185
Bulgari (Rome): 101 (centre right), 180 (top),
   183 (except top), 186 (except right centre)
Cartier Archives (Paris): 120, 163
Eleuteri, Carlo (Rome): 40 (bottom), 56 (top
   left), 59 (four centre pictures), 62, 63 (top
   left), 91, 99 (left), 108 (bottom), 113 (bottom
   left)
Fane, Harry: 154 (left)
Flockinger, Gerda (London): 189 (bottom)
Graff (London): 192
Grima, Andrew (London): 176 (left and centre)
Harris, Nicholas (London): 101 (top centre and
   right, centre right and bottom centre and
   right)
Lalaounis Collection: 187 (except bottom)
Marina B. (Geneva): 181 (except second row
   left)
Mauboussin Archives (Paris): 170 (upper right)
Mellerio Archives (Paris): 76–77 (upper three),
   104, 105 (except bottom right), 117 (right),
   118–119, 124 (except bottom left), 168
   (right), 169 (bottom left), 172 (bottom), 173,
   184 (right)
Phillips, S.J. (London): 49, 95, 106–107
   (centre)
Tiffany (New York): 178 (bottom) (Schlumberger Dept), 188, 189 (top)
Van Cleef & Arpels (Paris): 155 (left), 170
   (centre), 174–175 (four along top)
Verdura (New York): 175 (bottom left)
Winston, Harry (New York): 191 (top)
Zendrini (Rome): 164 (top)

Anonymous private collections
Geneva: 79 (bottom right), 97 (photo copyright
   Michael Oldford, New York)
London: 106 (right), 108 (top right), 50–51
   (centre), 64 (photo copyright Lucinda Dou-
   glas-Menzies, London).
New York: 199 (right centre), 123 (bottom
   right)

Publications
Vever, *La Bijouterie Française au XIXe siècle*,
   Paris, 1908: 78

Index

223